Administering
Christian Education

Administering Christian Education

Principles of Administration for Ministers and Christian Leaders

by

Robert K. Bower
Professor of Practical Theology
and Pastoral Counseling
Fuller Theological Seminary

Wm. B. Eerdmans Publishing Company
Grand Rapids, Michigan

Preface

This volume discusses the important and recurring problems which are found in the administration of a church Christian education program whether that program be in a church with a membership of two hundred or one with two thousand. It deals with those problems from the perspective of the pastor, the minister of Christian education (or the director of Christian education), and lay officials who assist the church staff in its teaching ministry; yet, it does not neglect the interests and concerns of other lay personnel such as teachers and youth sponsors. It is a manual not only of theory but also of practice; it stresses the *what*, the *why*, and the *how* of administration.

At the end of most of the chapters the reader will find references to administrative techniques which illustrate the principles which have been described and explained. No attempt, however, has been made to be comprehensive; rather, the aim has been to make the most significant contribution to the theme of the chapter without being repetitive. The techniques have been carefully selected and are drawn from actual church situations. Because of this, the reader is provided with a *realistic* application of theoretical principles to the educational work of the church. Through a study of the techniques, the reader should gain creative ideas for the development of a vital and dynamic Christian education program for his own church as well as for the improvement of any program which may presently exist.

The publication of this book should not have been realized except for the generous assistance and encouragement of many persons. In particular I want to express my gratitude to Mrs. Marjorie Long and Mrs. Madrene Bierma, whose secretarial help has been most invaluable. Thanks are also due to the many classes of students which have stimulated me as I have delivered much of this material in the form of lectures over the past ten years. Most of all, I wish to express my deep and heartfelt appreciation for the assistance and forbearance of my wife Jean during the writing and preparation of this manuscript.

—Robert K. Bower

Pasadena, California

Contents

APPENDIX
APPLIED ADMINISTRATIVE TECHNIQUES

List of Figures

I

Introduction

Importance of Administration

Expanded Educational Program Needed

The Supreme Court of the United States has rendered decisions which have in the opinion of many church officials contributed to a growing secularism within our country. To say that the church must double her educational efforts and become a bulwark against secular forces is but to declare what is already known. The handwriting on the wall can be read by each member of the church: a sound, consistent, and enlarged educational curriculum must be an integral part of every local church program if the church is to survive. A far better education in Christian beliefs and principles is needed than the church has previously provided its members, especially those who are in the formative years of life.

The thought of larger church educational programs, however, has begun to alarm ministers and laymen alike. The needs and problems of people continue to multiply though the resources and methods for the administration of constantly expanding programs are often lacking. Still, the continued growth of church programs seems inevitable. The need, therefore, for new knowledge in administrative techniques is all too apparent.

The program of Christian education usually comprises over half of a church's activities. A typically active church today may sponsor such groups and events as church school, youth

11

groups, vacation church school, summer youth camps, workers' conferences, released-time education, junior church, girls' and boys' clubs, extended sessions, scouts, and church membership classes. In addition to these, the necessity for thorough Christian instruction has now become so urgent that Protestant churches must seriously consider an even larger and more intensive program for laying a moral and spiritual foundation for their youth and adults. For years, Roman Catholic churches and Jewish synagogues have provided their people, particularly their youth, with just such programs and with great success. It is now time for those churches which claim the Protestant heritage to expand their educational programs far beyond their present offerings. A vital *and* a well-administered program is the need of today.

Despite the criticism which has been directed toward Christian education programs in the past — criticism aimed at weak administration, poor curriculums, inadequate facilities, and ineffective teaching — increasing numbers of young people and adults have been reached for Christ. History will show that the educational arm of the church has been a powerful instrument for building and strengthening the "household of faith." Whenever there has been faith in the educational program so that it has received strong support, the church has grown; whenever faith in the program has lagged, the church has remained static or declined.

Obviously, a Christian education program cannot run itself. There must be responsible persons who will administer it properly. The work of the church must be done "decently and in order." But without some knowledge of administrative methods, the result can only be one of inefficiency. A good church will fight against poorly planned and poorly executed programs. Good church members will demand good administration. Administrators must work with literally hundreds of details when directing a broad educational program. Plans must be made and policies formulated; they must be carefully implemented; data must be gathered indicating the extent to which the plans and policies are successful or unsuccessful, so that future policy-making and planning will point toward realistic goals. In essence, a sound program calls for effective administration.

Relation of Education and Administration to the Church

How do education and its accompanying administrative techniques relate to the church? To answer this question we must understand the nature of the church, which is the Body of Christ.

The Apostle Paul refers to the church both as visible and invisible, that is, to the church as an organism and as a local congregation (Eph. 1:22, 23; I Cor. 1:2). He recognizes the fact that the true and invisible church consists of those believers who at any time or place have accepted and shared in God's redemptive grace in Christ Jesus. In so far as the visible church is an expression of the will of her Lord, to that extent it is fulfilling its mission to "be" the church and is identified with the invisible church whose meaning, purpose, and existence are found in its Lord and Savior. The church on earth therefore is a congregation of the redeemed. It nurtures its members and instructs them in the love and worship of God. It is a redemptive community that witnesses through both word and action to the love of God for men. It is the instrument God uses for the proclamation of the gospel throughout the world.

For this ministry and mission, God has not left His church helpless or without spiritual resources. Rather, He has equipped the church with such gifts as it needs for growth and for reaching maturity. Preaching, teaching, evangelizing, and other spiritual gifts have been bestowed upon the church for the explicit purpose of helping her to fulfill her divine calling (Eph. 4:11ff.; I Cor. 12:28ff.). Sherrill states this in his volume *The Gift of Power* when he says that the church or Christian community is a *koinonia*, a fellowship between members who are capable of "becoming channels of the corrective, redemptive, and re-creative power of God. In such a society those who preach the Word of God and those who teach the Word of God are . . . . 'laborers together with God.' "[1]

From this we may infer that the teaching or educational ministry is given by the Holy Spirit in the form of a spiritual gift to the church so that it may fulfill its mission in Christ. The church, therefore, is subservient to Christ, who is its Head.

[1] Lewis J. Sherrill, *The Gift of Power*, p. 90.

The educational ministry in turn is subservient to, and part of, the church. If these things are so, then education and its accompanying administrative and instructional methodologies are not ends in themselves. They are simply *means* to the ends which God has ordained for His church. Teaching and all other gifts are for the purpose of serving the church, so that the church might serve Christ effectually.

Education *within* the church, then, exists to serve Christ and in so doing seeks, through administrative and other methods, to train leadership, to provide instructional facilities, to supply teachers, and to create the type of atmosphere which is most conducive to effective learning.

Efficient administration, in a context of education which is properly related to the church, can contribute to the development of a curriculum that will truly "educate" the student. Inefficient administration, on the other hand, will cheat the student in a hundred ways and deprive him of the dynamic and spiritual program which he deserves.

Of course, there are some people who would prefer to abolish administrative responsibilities from the church altogether, at least for the minister if for no one else. They point to the vast amount of time he already spends on administrative matters. His predicament has been described by McCann in *The Churches and Mental Health*:

> In a one-clergyman parish, the minister appears to be a kind of 'general manager,' but is actually required by subtle demands, to be his own committee of specialists. Shortcomings in any of the six central roles — administrator, organizer, pastor, preacher, priest, teacher — can undermine his over-all effectiveness. As administrator, the minister must often supervise the financial program of the church and coordinate the work of its staff. As organizer, he must participate in intra- and inter-denominational activities and be active in community affairs. As pastor, he serves his congregants in a person-to-person relationship. As priest, he administers sacraments, conducts marriages, funerals, and other rites of passage, and leads in services of worship. As preacher, he tries to provide guidance and inspiration in a one-to-many relationship with his parishioners. As teacher, he directs the church's religious education program and 'teaches' in many other less defined ways.[2]

[2] Richard V. McCann, *The Churches and Mental Health*, p. 41.

14

The author, then, states that the average minister devotes fifty per cent of his time to organizational and administrative duties, much of which is obviously connected with the church's educational program.

Those who would dispense with all administration in a church usually fall into three general categories: first, those who are uninformed about the magnitude of the program in many churches; second, those who are informed about its size but know little about directing and coordinating the activities of hundreds of persons simultaneously; and third, those who have witnessed inefficient administration in *their* church and generalize from this, concluding that all other churches have equally poor administration and that nothing can be done to improve the situation.

It would undoubtedly be possible to eliminate boards, committees, superintendents, and group sponsors, but such an action would set the church back many generations to the days when most young people (as well as most adults) were found outside the church rather than in it.[3] Instead of taking a radical and backward step of this kind, ministers and others charged with the direction of church educational programs should acquire additional information about, and develop skills in, administrative techniques, so that other personnel may be trained to help shoulder the administrative load effectively. Thus, *better* administration is the need of the hour, *not* its abolition. Improving administration, however, calls for an emphasis upon both sound practice and its theoretical undergirdings.

Theory in Administration

Necessity for Theory

Are pastors in our churches interested in acquiring more information about efficient administrative processes? Fairchild and Wynn report that of the ten categories in which pastors seek more instruction, three categories involve administration, with one of the three (that of leadership recruitment and train-

[3] See p. 17 for church membership figures in the past.

ing) ranking second.[4] It would appear, then, that ministers are keenly aware of their need for guidance in administrative theory and practice.

But why has this need become so pressing in our day? One reason that may be given is that, in the United States, the population in rural areas (where the vast majority of smaller churches exist) is now undergoing a drastic change, with a marked shift in population from these areas to the cities. In 1900, approximately 70 per cent of the population lived in the rural areas of our country with some 30 per cent living in the urban areas. Today we find these percentages almost reversed. We have a nation of great cities. With the influx of hundreds of thousands of persons into the cities, urban churches were forced into a choice between establishing a number of branch or mission churches to accommodate the newcomers or of expanding their own church plants. Because it was often considered much simpler to enlarge existing churches, this pattern was followed in a great many cases. "Since 1926 the average membership per local church (parish, congregation) of all religious bodies has been increasing. In 1926 the figure was 235; by 1950, it was 304; and by 1960, 359"[5] — an increase of over 52 per cent.

The trend toward larger institutions has also been noticeable in the public school systems of our country in which the smaller schools, particularly the traditional "little, red, one-room schoolhouses" have been gradually eliminated in favor of more efficient school plants consisting of many classrooms and instructional personnel. Consolidation has been, and continues to be, the trend in both church and public school life. Indeed, it may be observed in almost every area of our contemporary culture (note, for example, the mergers now occurring in the business world).

As a result of this consolidating process, large churches in ever-increasing numbers appeared, many of which claimed memberships running into the thousands. Along with the rise of the

[4] Roy W. Fairchild and John C. Wynn, *Families in the Church*, p. 234.
[5] Office of Publication and Distribution, edited by Benson Y. Landis, *Edition for 1962 Yearbook of American Churches*, National Council of Churches of Christ in the USA, p. 276.

large urban churches came the logical demand for men who knew how to coordinate effectively the activities of the officers, teachers, and general membership in the programs of the churches.

A second reason is that Americans are becoming more and more church conscious. This is not to say that American Christianity is any more vital than it once was (though we would like to believe that it is). It is but to say that a greater proportion of the total population now claims church membership than in previous decades. In 1850, some 16 per cent of the population was recorded on church membership rolls. By 1950 this percentage had surged to 57 per cent[6] and by 1960 it had reached over 63 per cent.[7] Thus, the proportion of the population now claiming membership in the churches of our country is higher than in any previous generation.

A third reason for an increased interest in more efficient administration in our churches is that the principle of separation of church and state in our country has relegated the major responsibility for the moral and spiritual training of our youth to the churches[8] — a responsibility which in other countries is usually shared by the public school systems. Although the public schools have manifested some degree of interest in character training,[9] this has been nominal at most, and after the home, it is the churches which must carry the *primary* obligation of training youth in moral values and in developing the spiritual dimension of their personalities. Consequently, Christian education has moved in the opinion of many from a secondary ministry to a primary one in the churches of the United States.

To the great challenge of educating America's children in moral and spiritual values, the churches have responded with expanded programs, including through-the-week religious activities. In some instances, a rather sizable staff is required to plan and coordinate the Sunday and weekday activities in the Christian education program. The First Presbyterian Church of Hollywood, California, stands unique among the churches

6 *Ibid.,* (1956 *Yearbook*), p. 266.
7 *Ibid.,* p. 275.
8 See also page 11.
9 See the volume put out by the Educational Policies Commission, *Moral and Spiritual Values in the Public Schools,* National Education Association, Washington, D.C., 1951.

in that the enrollment of its church school is over 5,500, requiring more than 500 teachers and workers! Thus it is no surprise when a church administering a program for several thousand members begins to take on the appearance of a vast organizational enterprise. A business with several thousand employees would require no little amount of administrative ability. And to be without a knowledge of administrative principles in an organization of such great size would lead to disorder, confusion, endless turmoil, and frustration for all concerned.

It becomes necessary, therefore, for pastors and other staff members of large and even moderately large churches to develop a theory of organization and administration which is comprehensive, effective, and in harmony with Christian principles.

Basic Concepts for Improved Administrative Theory

Suggestions for the improvement of administrative techniques in our churches will be based largely upon certain fundamental considerations. These considerations may be openly expressed or simply implied. But the reader should be aware that such considerations (primary ideas or assumptions) do exist and influence to no small degree the relationships which are set up between the principles described and the conclusions drawn. Some of the assumptions which are intrinsic to the theoretical principles described in the subsequent chapters are these:

(1) *Persons are more important than the organization.* This is not only a "democratic" principle derived from our Western culture, but it comes from the Bible itself. The individual was more important to our Lord than was the visible organized church of His day. And we believe that the church of Jesus Christ today can be the church in the true sense of the word only when it has elevated the interests of the individual above those of the external visible church. In other words, we must never sacrifice the individual for the sake of organizational efficiency.

(2) *Each person in the Body of Christ has a function or ministry to perform.* In I Corinthians 12, Paul clearly indicates that the members of the Body are interdependent and are important to its proper functioning. The responsibility of the adminis-

trator, therefore, becomes that of identifying the place in which each member may serve in the church and thereby increase its effectiveness and its mission.

(3) *The ultimate aim of church leaders should be that of serving rather than that of being served.* Christ has set the example for all who desire to exercise leadership in the church. He has said that whosoever would be "first among you must be your slave; even as the Son of man came not to be served but to serve, and to give his life as a ransom for many" (Matt. 20:27). He Himself not only taught this principle but exemplified it in His own life and ministry. Paul spoke of himself as the servant of Jesus Christ (Rom. 1:1) and as a servant of the Corinthian church (II Cor. 4:5). The Christian leader, then, should develop an image of himself not as a dictator but as a servant.

(4) *Leaders must be willing to accept responsibility for directing the program.* Although it may appear to be paradoxical, the leader must take the attitude of one who serves and yet of one who is willing to assume responsibility for directing and supervising the activities of personnel assigned to him, even as Christ, who served, also instructed and sent His disciples out with directives to evangelize the world. Administration and supervision become matters of guiding, directing, and helping others in their ministry for Christ. It is direction of a program, however, through planning and through educational supervisory means rather than through authoritarian and dictatorial methods.

(5) *A clearly defined organization is essential.* The Apostle Paul tells us that there were church officials who were appointed to carry out general tasks within the church. Bishops and deacons, as well as apostles, prophets, and evangelists, were set apart for their particular ministries. Everything was to be done decently and in order (I Cor. 14:40). The exact nature of the organization beyond the broadly described structure given in the New Testament epistles is not provided for us.[10] It is undoubtedly best to make certain that all of the New Testament ministries of a universal nature are an integral part of any church organization. But not every detail is provided in the New

[10] Alan Richardson, *An Introduction to the Theology of the New Testament*, p. 312.

Testament. For example, there is no indication of Sunday school teachers, pianists, custodians, or bus drivers. That *some* type of organization was needed so that the activities would be "done decently and in order" was the important consideration.

(6) *All positions in the church are important.* Of necessity we shall be referring to some positions in the organization as being "higher" or "lower." This is not to say that in the eyes of God one ministry or position is more important than another. As Paul has said: ". . . the parts of the body which seem to be weaker are indispensable, and those parts of the body which we think less honorable we invest with the greater honor" (I Cor. 12:22, 23). However, the Bible *does* make distinctions between various duties. We find, for example, Moses' father-in-law, Jethro, speaking of the *small* matters and the *great* matters, the latter to be settled by Moses (Exod. 18:22). Even the apostles distinguished between what seemed to be the more important duties and those which were less important (Acts 6:1-4). It will, therefore, be necessary to differentiate between the types of administrative work; yet, in the final analysis, the reader must remember that it is the faithfulness to one's appointed duties which is of ultimate value, not what position is held, nor how important from man's standpoint one's work seems to be to the organization.

General Administrative Operations

Over the years, a general body of principles has been developed by administrators for guiding themselves in their actions and decisions. Ministers and other church officials should seriously consider adopting the administrative methods which have already been proven of value in the field and are in harmony with the ideals of Scripture. If one wishes, he may develop his own set of principles through trial and error; many have attempted in the past to do this, but not without making costly errors and creating long-term difficulties. Is it not much better to profit from the experience of men who have developed and tested modern principles of organization and administration over a period of a lifetime? Furthermore, the principles of which we speak have been derived from a number of broad areas including the commercial, the military, and the ecclesiastical.

Occasionally, the reader will find administrative principles referred to in the literature as hypotheses or theories, but whatever word is employed for their identification, they make up a pattern of operation which is followed rather uniformly by most successful organizations. This pattern of behavior can be broken down into a number of general rules which the administrator should follow whether he be a pastor, a foreman or a corporation president.

Pfiffner,[11] Tead,[12] Urwick,[13] and others have spelled out many of the general rules which have guided successful administrators in their executive duties. The rules and operational concepts which they have developed and which we shall study in some detail in the following chapters are:

(1) *Planning.* This general concept emphasizes the need to forecast or predict the future and to develop one's program accordingly. A most crucial aspect of the entire planning process is that of policy-making — a subject which will become increasingly important to the administrator as his organization enlarges.

(2) *Organizing.* How does one go about arranging personnel so that they are suitably related to each other, so that they understand to whom they are responsible and from whom they may receive assistance? *This* is the task of organization. It is occupied primarily with the proper arrangement of individuals with their concomitant authorities and responsibilities within an institution.

(3) *Delegating.* One of the most important administrative activities is that of assigning specific duties to others. No leader, no administrator, can do everything. He must learn to delegate some of his work to other persons and then permit them to carry out their duties without interference in so far as the assigned work is performed satisfactorily.

(4) *Staffing.* Perhaps the most difficult administrative task today in the churches is that of persuading persons to accept

---

11 John Pfiffner, *The Supervision of Personnel,* pp. 47-48.
12 Ordway Tead, *The Art of Administration,* Chap. 7.
13 Lyndall Urwick, *Elements of Administration,* pp. 16-20.

leadership responsibility for major areas of the Christian education program. Recruitment, preparation, and the retention of leaders for this program are processes included in the concept of "staffing."

(5) *Coordinating.* It is one thing to arrange the personnel in a church effectively, but it is an entirely different matter to coordinate their activities so that they are efficient in their respective operations. The various coordinating devices available to the administrator for skillful operation are described under this term.

(6) *Controlling.* Some administrators prefer to divide this administrative concept into two aspects: reporting and budgeting. For the purpose of this volume, however, we shall use this concept, which is more inclusive than either of its two aspects. The essential thought in "controlling" is that of continuous evaluation (or "checking") to see that plans are carried out properly.

Typical Problems of Administration

General Problems

What are some of the recurring problems in Christian education with which administrators are concerned? That is, what are the operations which demand constant attention and the application of administrative principles if programs are to be successful? The following list is not exhaustive but merely suggestive of those operations in which administrators are involved. They are expected to make up budgets, supervise expenditures of large sums of money (usually with board approval), evaluate the work of the leaders, keep members informed of the program, install an adequate record system, direct the visitation program (or assist in its coordination), recruit new leaders, train teachers, assist delegates with their assignments, set up organizational charts, interview prospective leaders for positions on the educational staff, formulate policies, assist in working out program details and special projects; in short, provide a comprehensive type of leadership that is an essential and vital contribution to the ministry of the church.

Democratic or Autocratic Administration?

One major problem facing our churches is whether to employ democratic or autocratic administrative processes. The author believes that democratic processes are those best suited to the churches because they more adequately reflect the Christian position and its concepts of "the dignity and importance of the individual," "the equality of every person," and "the right of liberty and freedom for the human personality" — all of which are an integral part of democratic administrative theory. When one speaks of democratic administration, he places the greatest emphasis on the *person* in administration rather than on the *process*, though one should recognize that these are so intimately related that they can be separated only for literary purposes. Administrative processes do not exist apart from persons, nor do persons in an organization operate without some kind of administrative procedures, regardless of how inconsistent or inefficient these may be. Tead has emphasized both of these aspects of administration by saying that there must be an expert concern for process and material things *and* a concern for persons and human relations.[14] This concern for both persons and process seems to be the one emphasis now emerging from research in the field of organization and administration. We mean by this that there has been a marked shift from an extreme form of democratic administration. Pfiffner and Sherwood[15] have noted this change when they write that it is now questionable whether the totally democratic approach can be made to fit our general modes of organization. They also state that it is becoming quite apparent from later research that too much employee-centeredness can result in low morale. The result is that administrative theory is now moving toward a middle ground, sometimes called "reality-oriented" leadership. This modified democratic approach avoids the pitfalls of the extreme form of democratic administration (which tends to ignore institutional goals) and also opens up the possibility of bringing together the goals of the church and her individual members on a much more realistic basis.

14 Ordway Tead, *op. cit.*, p. 104.
15 John M. Pfiffner and Frank P. Sherwood, *Administrative Organization*, 1960, p. 368.

Note on the Use of Special Terms

In this book the terms "administrator," "leader," "pastor," "church executive," "minister," "minister of Christian education," and "director of Christian education" will be used interchangeably. We shall use the expressions "Sunday school," "church school," and "Sunday church school," in much the same way, since these titles are in common use in one section of our country or another. Also, because churches differ in their organizational structure, we shall use the terms "Board of Christian Education," and "Committee of Christian Education" interchangeably. In the event that a church has neither of these groups in its organization, the reader should substitute the title of that group which carries the responsibility for the general planning of the Christian education program.

II

Organization

Men are social creatures. They gather together either in-
stinctively or out of necessity not only because they desire
socializing experiences but also because they have found that
more can be accomplished through group than through individual
efforts. There are always projects and objectives confronting
an individual which he recognizes cannot be achieved without
the assistance of others. If he persuades another person (or
several persons) to cooperate with him in the achievement of a
particular objective, he has, in effect, established an organization
which is social in nature, though it may indeed be limited in
size.

Chester Barnard, an extensive writer in the field of business
administration, states that an organization exists when three
general factors are present: (1) communication between persons,
(2) a willingness to serve on the part of these persons, and (3)
a common purpose or goal which unifies or coordinates their
efforts.[1]

The simplest organization in Barnard's terms would be two
persons in communication working toward a common goal.
The permanence of an organization, however, depends upon
the willingness of the personnel to continue their service. This
in turn is dependent upon their faith in the organization's goal
or major purpose. But whenever sacrifices exceed satisfactions,

---

[1] Chester I. Bernard, *The Functions of the Executive*, p. 82.

25

willingness tends to disappear.[2] Thus, a well-known foundation, set up for the unique purpose of combating poliomyelitis,
found that people greatly reduced their contributions to the
foundation when the Salk vaccine was announced. In the public's eye, the unique objective of the foundation — that of fighting
and defeating polio — had been achieved, though there were
literally thousands of polio victims who could never profit from
this great discovery since they had contracted the disease before
the new vaccine was made available. Thus, continued funds
were needed to care for these victims. Financial support,
however, diminished sharply and the foundation was forced to
cut back on many of its services and close down several of its
facilities. In the eyes of the general public, the unique and primary objective of the foundation had been achieved, namely,
the defeat of polio. But apparently the objective of continued
therapy for those who had developed polio prior to the discovery
of the vaccine did not sufficiently stimulate donors, who felt that
the sacrifices (which were largely psychological and humani-
tarian in nature) exceeded the satisfactions derived from the act
of giving to a needy and worthwhile cause.

Likewise, if the primary goal of the church does not appear to
be a unique and sufficiently worthy one, then its members also
may feel that the sacrifices exceed the satisfactions. Churches,
for instance, which claim only social or educational objectives
as their unique work may discover that welfare agencies and
educational institutions are providing a superior type of service
in these areas, a service beyond that which the churches themselves can offer. When this is the case, church members tend to
question the primary function of the church and the demands it
places upon their time and money. The sacrifices which people
must make to conduct a comprehensive church program can indeed be great, even to the extent of involving all of their time,
money, and energy which are over and above that required to
meet the necessities of life.

We must ask, then, What *is* the church's unique goal? What
is this purpose that binds people together so that the church
has continued and still continues to exist? The church, of

2 *Ibid.* p. 82.

course, should not attempt to seek a goal that will justify its existence, but the goal should be part of the church's very nature and genesis.

Since our Lord is the source and origin of the church, His goal must become the church's goal. And that goal is the reconciliation of men to God, the reunion whereby man tastes of the redemption God has wrought in His Son and receives the gift of life eternal. *This* is the unique function and purpose of the church. Because this goal does not duplicate the work of other organizations or institutions, the church has a reason for her existence. The work of reconciliation has been given to the church exclusively by her Lord. As long as people recognize that this goal is a supremely important and justifiable one, and as long as they see others committing their lives to Jesus Christ as Lord and Savior, the spiritual satisfactions derived should far exceed the material sacrifices which must be made. Let us not forget, therefore, that the most important part of any organization's program is its unique goal, its major purpose. This purpose must be clearly understood by the members of an organization if there is to be a spirit of mission and if there are to be the necessary sacrifices.

Meaning of Organization

The term "organization" is used in several ways by those working in the field of administration. When one hears the expression, "Let's get things organized around here!" it may refer to the need for improved *coordination* of activities. Or, it may be a demand for something more basic, namely, a demand for defining the jobs to be done and relating these to each other so that a definite structure is established. When people know what their positions and responsibilities are, then they can begin to coordinate their actions. The prerequisite, however, for good coordination is a structure in which people know what their definite place is in the organization and what their specific duties are.

Because the task of *setting up* an organization (involving as it does the determination of the offices to be established and a description of their accompanying responsibilities) is such a sizable undertaking, it is best not to "overload" it by including

27

the process of coordination. We shall, therefore, employ Newman's definition:

> The administrative process of *organizing* an enterprise or any of its parts consists of (1) *dividing and grouping the work* that should be done (including administration) into individual jobs, and (2) defining the established *relationships* between individuals filling these jobs.[3]

In line with the above, the term "organization" will refer primarily to the administrative activity of setting up the general structure of an enterprise and arranging the jobs within that structure in vertical and horizontal relationships according to a general pattern. On the other hand, when we speak of *facilitating* the operations within a structure so that they function smoothly and efficiently, we shall employ the term "coordination."

Occasionally a person will claim that a study of organization and its attendant principles is of little value to the church with limited membership. Newman,[4] however, says that organization is essential to small as well as to large enterprises. Moreover, is it not true that the God who has admonished the church to be orderly would also expect churches both large and small to be well ordered, well arranged, and systematic in their operation?

Analyzing the Organization of an Existing Church

One of the best methods for discovering the organizational structure of a church is to conduct a careful, analytical study of existing interpersonal relationships. But how does one proceed to conduct such a study? Where should one begin?

Perhaps the most rewarding method involves, first of all, a close study of the church constitution. The student should identify the groups to which the constitution grants ultimate authority for the operation of at least four areas of church life: the legal, the financial, the educational, and the spiritual. The spiritual area, however, is more inclusive in scope and should not be interpreted as mutually exclusive from the others. In practice, all the officers and members connected with a particular

[3] William H. Newman, *Administrative Action*, p. 123.
[4] *Ibid.*

area are responsible for the general spiritual welfare of the church.

When the groups responsible for the general areas of the church's life have been identified, a good beginning toward understanding church organization will have been made. Usually, one will find listed such groups as the Official Board, the Session, the Trustees, the Board of Christian Education, the Board of Deacons, etc. Particular note of the responsibilities and the authority of each of these groups should be made. In fact, all boards and committees of both a permanent and temporary nature should be analyzed in this way.

In the constitution of most churches, the relationships of the pastor to the church, to the staff, and to all of the official groups within the church will be given in more or less detail. Occasionally, the relationships are not specifically given but are only implied. A great deal of vital information describing existing general relationships can, nevertheless, be obtained through this kind of investigation. This same procedure should be followed in respect to each person in a position of responsibility, so that all of the complex relationships can eventually be diagrammed and put into the form of an organizational chart.

After the church constitution has been analyzed, further analyses should be made of other constitutions which may exist in the church. We refer to those constitutions which are associated with the work of the Sunday church school, youth groups, and other church organizations.

The final operation is to diagram as clearly as possible the relationships which exist between all important groups and personnel so that the channels of responsibility and communication are easily discernible. In making up such a drawing, (a) all lines should be vertical or horizontal (all slanted lines should be avoided if possible), (b) lines indicating authority should be solid; cooperative relationships or optional items should employ broken lines, (c) groups of equal authority should be placed on the same level and those with greater authority placed closer to the top of the chart, and (d) the principle of unity of management should be followed at as many points as possible, i.e., a person should be responsible to only one administrative superior or supervisor (see Figure 1). A model for setting up charts is provided in Figure 2.

If an organizational chart is to be drawn up by a church for the first time, it is usually best to make such a chart tentative in nature. Figure 3 is an example of this type of chart for a Congregational or Baptist form of church government. The use of the word "tentative" at this stage is important; otherwise, an attitude may develop among the people to the effect that an organizational strait jacket is being forced upon them, limiting their activities and their personal freedom. There is little doubt that this feeling has some basis, in fact, for those who may have exercised more authority than they rightfully deserve or more than was originally intended by the church. A chart may easily become a threat to them because their prestige rating appears to be at stake. In order to avoid suspicion or jealousy (though such ought not to exist in the house of God), it is the better part of wisdom to draw up only tentative charts at the beginning. Moreover, relationships which deserve to be included in an organizational chart may be overlooked on a first analysis, and for this reason also the "tentative" chart is the advisable one to employ in the preliminary stages. A permanent chart may require several years of study but if it is the result of careful, cooperative, and painstaking analysis, it should receive widespread acceptance. (Examples of permanent-type charts are given in Figures 4 and 5.) In any event, it is well to remember that after an organizational relationship has been put into print it is most difficult to revise. This is one of the disadvantages of charts. For this reason it is well to proceed slowly and cautiously until a truly acceptable chart has been drawn up and approved.

DIRECTED BY ONE SUPERVISOR

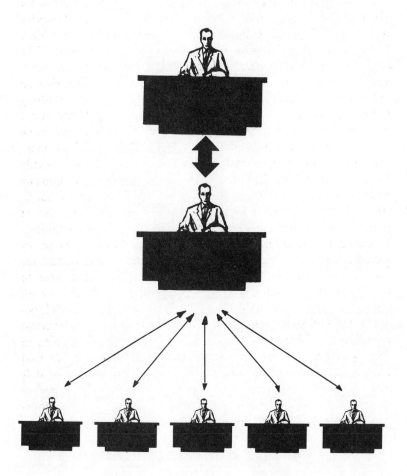

Report to One Supervisor

Figure 1.   Illustration of Unity of Management Principle.   Source: *Management Course for Air Force Supervisors*, U.S. Government Printing Office, 1955, Part 3, p. 24.

CHARTING THE STRUCTURE

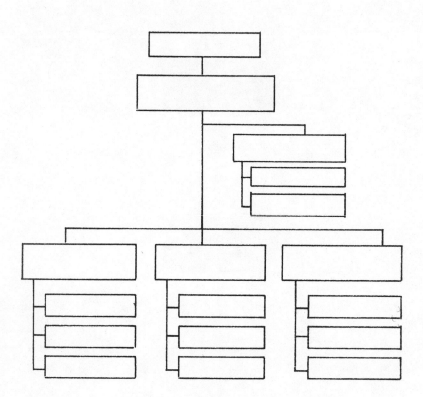

Line and Staff Organization

Figure 2. Model for Setting Up an Organizational Chart. Source: *Management Course for Air Force Supervisors*, U.S. Government Printing Office, 1955, Part 3, p. 23.

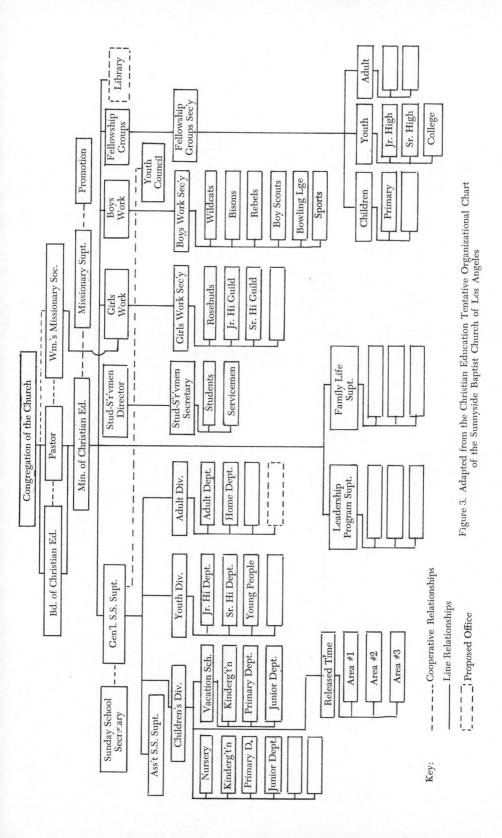

Figure 3. Adapted from the Christian Education Tentative Organizational Chart of the Sunnyside Baptist Church of Los Angeles

Key:
    – – – – – Cooperative Relationships
    ————— Line Relationships
    ⌐ ¬ Proposed Office

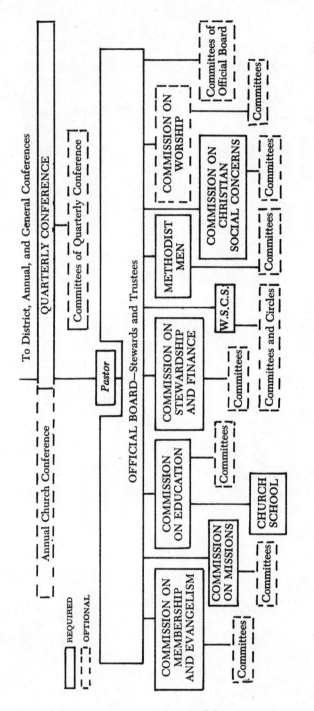

ORGANIZATION DIAGRAM, THE LOCAL CHURCH

Figure 4.   Methodist Church Organization. Source: *Methodist Officers Handbook* by Ramp, Abingdon Press, 1961, p. 48

34

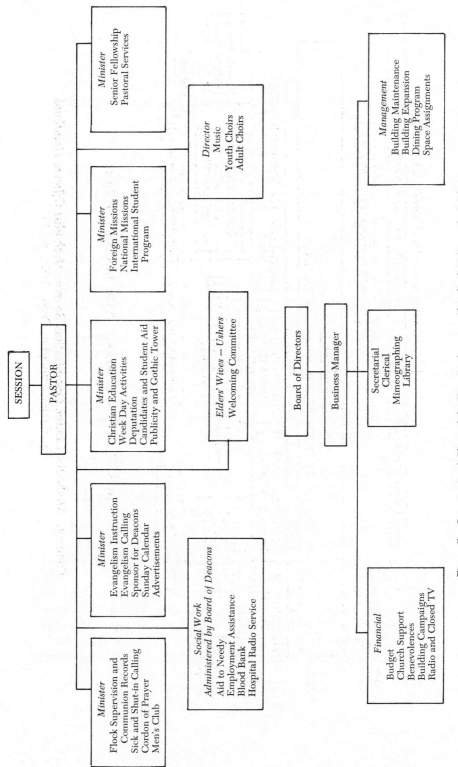

Figure 5. Organizational Chart of the First Presbyterian Church of Hollywood, California

The advantages of a published chart usually outweigh its disadvantages. Sears has described the advantages of charts (and also manuals and handbooks in written or published form) in these words:

> It [a chart, or a handbook] carries loads that otherwise would have to be carried in memory and that would have to be sure to be recalled at every proper time and place. It does even more than this; it keeps facts, definitions, divisions of labor, purposes, plans, procedures, all defined in unchanging terms. Paper organizations never forget; they have no selfish motives, no pride in getting more power. They are never lazy or mean or indifferent, and they need not be stupid. It is true that at times they crystallize things that should be kept elastic, and, at times, may even prevent growth; but they need not do these evil things. Their virtue is consistency, continuity, completeness, permanence, readiness for action — all bases for common understanding[5]

Charts and other similar devices, therefore, help institutional personnel to see relationships, indeed, to visualize in pictorial form their relationships to others in the organization's structure. Furthermore, if they can acquire an insight into the basic components of institutions, they should eventually develop a total and comprehensive view of their own organizations. Briefly, the basic components are these: the line function, the staff function, the informal function, and the external communication function.

Let us now look at these in detail.

The Line Function

This is known in organizational theory as the vertical aspect of organization. Anyone who holds a position in the line is one who has been given authority to issue commands, orders, and directives which significantly influence the entire organization. The commands or directives issued by line personnel always affect those who function at, and below, the level at which the orders are issued. For example, an army line officer can order an entire unit to embark for some distant point. His order will affect all of the officers and enlisted men in that unit. Line officials, whether in the Armed Forces or in the nonmilitary world, therefore, direct, make decisions, and carry general

[5] Jesse B. Sears, *The Nature of the Administrative Process*, pp. 92-93.

responsibility for the success or failure of an organization's program. Allen stipulates this when he says: "Line managers have authority to accept, reject, or modify the advice or service proffered by the staff."[6]

The Staff Function

The second aspect of organization is that of the staff. This is the horizontal aspect of organization. It does not issue commands, but simply offers advice to those functioning in the line. The staff is tied into the line only in an *advisory* capacity. Whatever authority staff members exercise is derived from their technical and specialized knowledge and therefore is commonly spoken of as the "right arm" of the line personnel.[7] Staff members carry the responsibility for gathering and tabulating data and suggesting alternative plans for achieving a specific objective. Line members, on the other hand, must select the relevant data provided and interpret these, weigh the alternative plans suggested, and then make those decisions which will result in the most effectual approach to the attainment of stated objectives. The staff proposes, therefore, and the line judges. Again, as Allen has indicated:

> Staff should offer its advice and service where it believes it is needed and without being specifically invited. It is not necessary for staff to wait to be called. It should keep itself informed about the problems confronting the line, think ahead, make constructive plans and help the line solve its difficult operating problems.[8]

If a plan is successful, the line personnel receive the credit for its selection even though the staff may have developed it. But

[6] Louis A. Allen, *Management and Organization*, p. 248.

[7] One caution should be noted here in reference to terminology. "Staff" in the formal sense is that aspect which offers advice. However, when we speak of a "church staff," we generally use the term somewhat differently. Although the pastor may be referred to as a part of the "church staff," in actual practice he may function *both* in the line and in the staff in the organizational sense, directing the activities of associate ministers, clerks, typists and others, and also advising church boards. The official legislative body of the church and the church staff more closely resemble the Congress and the President's Cabinet with their respective responsibilities of legislation and execution.

[8] *Ibid.*

it is also true that if a plan fails in its purpose, the staff does not receive the major criticism though it may have developed and recommended the plan. It is the line personnel who must accept the responsibility for any failure inasmuch as it is their function to select workable plans and reject all others.

The Informal Function

Oftentimes, informal social groups are not included in an organizational chart. These groups may evolve slowly, almost imperceptibly, from within the organization until they become an integral though still informal part of the structure. Some executives have referred to these groups as "kitchen cabinets" because of the policies which they develop on a very unofficial basis. Being closely knit groups they will often meet informally at a group member's home to make plans which ultimately wield a great deal of influence. The term "clique" is frequently applied to such organized bodies. Since they may devise plans of action which catch the administrator off guard, he will be wise to identify and understand the nature of all such groups at the earliest possible time. Should these be broken up? Not always. Cliques and informal groups are not, in every case, detrimental to the welfare of an organization or a church. In discussing informal organizational groups, Dalton comments that:

> Informal action may work for many ends: to change and preserve the organization, to protect weak individuals, punish erring ones, reward others, to recruit new personnel, and to maintain dignity of the formal [organization].[9]

Take the case of a church which is located in a community with a high population turnover and a comparable turnover in the church membership. Cliques and informal groups in this type of situation form a "core of leadership" and thereby provide a source of stability and strength for a church in the midst of its changing constituency. Were it not for such groups, churches located in changing communities or in other similar situations might well find themselves without capable leadership, thereby

[9] Melville Dalton, *Men Who Manage*, p. 222.

jeopardizing their important ministry. It becomes essential then for administrators to study a church's organizational structure in reference to informal groups as well as the formal. Wherever informal groups are found, plans should be made to use them in a constructive way whenever possible, to use their spirit of cohesiveness, and to direct their efforts so that they, in effect, assist the formal groups in the achievement of the church's objectives.

External Communication Function

A fourth aspect of organization is the external channel of communication which exists, for the most part, outside the line and staff structures. In the United States Army the Inspector General serves in this capacity. The man at the lowest level of the Army may fail to obtain a hearing by those who are at the higher organizational levels. Whenever he tries to communicate with those who are above his immediate superior, there may be delay or a deliberate refusal to transmit the message to those persons authorized to make changes or grant requests. Consequently, the Inspector General often acts as a liaison between those at the higher organizational levels and those in the lower ranks so that any possible injustices may be rectified. Army personnel, therefore, are permitted to go directly to an Inspector General and explain their problems to him. If he feels that their complaints are justified, he has the authority to approach any officer or person in the hierarchy as a means of solving the problems which may have arisen.

Personnel managers in large corporations serve in much the same way. Assuming that they function efficiently as external channels of communication, their presence can mean a great deal in maintaining a high level of morale and an *esprit de corps* among those on the lower organizational levels. In reference to the church, the problem of communicating with those at the upper levels of a church organizational structure may not exist to the extent that it does in the United States Army or a business corporation, yet ministers should make themselves sufficiently available so that no "external channel of communication" is needed. An "open-door policy" should exist in every church regardless of size. The pastor and other officials, therefore, should be available for consultation and never give the appearance of being "too busy" to assist those urgently in need of help.

Methods Commonly Employed for Grouping Personnel

After one has grasped the four basic aspects of organization structure — viz., line, staff, informal functions, external functions — he should then be prepared to further his understanding through an identification of the methods which have been used for grouping or classifying personnel within the structure.

Historically speaking, grouping (sometimes referred to as departmentation) is carried on in one of five ways, or in various combinations of these.

There is grouping by process or function. Teaching (e.g., in the Sunday school), directing a choir, or coordinating the activities of some group are processes which are used for the purpose of grouping organizational personnel into teachers, directors, or coordinators. Grouping may also be done with reference to persons served. In this method, reference is made to the groups receiving special service — for example: the children's department, the youth department, or the adult department. The grouping of personnel in an organization may, however, be accomplished by reference to geography or to place. This is a rather common method for church groups which carry on a nationwide ministry. Thus there may be a Western and an Eastern Office of Christian Education for a church or denomination. At the level of the local church, there may be the simple procedure of identifying a group by the place at which it meets, for example, the *Tower* Class, or the *Fireside* Class. A further method of grouping is by time. Frequently there are names or descriptive phrases employed which indicate the time at which a group meets rather than the place of its meeting or the particular age group or persons served. An example of grouping by time would be the *Daily Vacation* Bible School, or the *Week-*

day Released Time Program. Grouping may also be accomplished by reference to the devices or instruments used by persons. In this category we have listed the organist, the file clerk, and the switchboard operator.

Upson has indicated that many organizations will employ a combination of methods. He says:

> The Roman Empire and the Roman Catholic Church organized or organize (with certain modifications) by geographical areas and then by functions within the areas. Our Federal Government and most governments for that matter reverse the process — organize first by functions and then in scores of instances administer those functions geographically.[10]

Thus in our Federal Government we have a number of these methods of grouping used rather extensively. The Internal Revenue Service (*process* of collecting taxes), the Veterans Administration (*persons* served), Department of the Air Force (*geographical* connotation by reference to location, i.e., the air) are examples.

In order to achieve unity of operation, all of these methods of organization should come under one office or person at each organizational level. In the case of our Federal Government, it is the Office of the President that provides the unity. In the Roman Catholic Church it is the Papal Office. In Protestant groups, at the local church level, it may be a chairman, a pastor, or a moderator. In each case, unity is achieved through the use of one person at the head of the organization, whatever its nature may be. Admittedly, some organizations appear to achieve unity of management through a group rather than a single person. In such cases cooperation, understanding, and dedication to a purpose must be present on a high level, otherwise ineffectiveness and inefficiency will result.[11]

---

[10] Lent D. Upson, *Letters on Public Administration,* p. 11.

[11] There is no desire to simplify some of the matters indicated here, but the reader should note that those organizations which are considered efficient are directed not by a group but by one person. The author is fully aware that there is a system of checks and balances in our Federal Government through the legislative, executive and judicial branches. But ultimately there is a high degree of unity for the nation through the action of the President, particularly in times of national emergency.

Rules for Organizing

The New Organization

How does one go about the organization of an institution? It may not be a matter of identifying an existing organizational structure but rather setting up a new one. Some executives prefer to organize from the top down and others from the bottom up. There seems to be little doubt about the necessity of beginning at the top level when a new organization is being established, since top-level personnel usually provide the plans and directions for those who are, or will be, part of the organization. Without sufficient leadership from the top, a new organization will lack coordination and the necessary stability for successful operation. Thus, leadership at the upper levels of the organization is concerned with such matters as organizing line and staff relationships, planning activities, setting policies, determining the availability of future leadership, and defining the duties of present leadership personnel.

What can be done, however, if no qualified person can be found to fill an important top-level position? Many administrators have followed the policy of keeping a position open until a well-qualified person appears, instead of selecting an incompetent person who will have to be removed from his office (and usually with much difficulty) at a later date. One pastor deferred the selection of a Sunday-school superintendent for an extended period of time. Meanwhile he, himself, served in that capacity because he realized the great difficulty that would ensue were the church to attempt the removal of an ineffective superintendent. His theory was that the cause of Christ would be better served if the position were left open until a qualified man was either discovered or trained.

In organizing an institution, some administrators study the aptitudes and capabilities of individuals first and then create positions in accord with their findings. This often produces a variety of "unique" jobs but tends to defeat the principle of organizational simplicity. It is usually considered far better to identify the jobs which are required for the most effective operation of the church, and then elect men to these positions.

The advantages of this approach are to be found in the relative stability of an organization year after year under these circumstances, and in the facility with which men can be trained for jobs which have been vacated. Changes in personnel, therefore, should not require accompanying changes in the number and types of positions. Of course there are always exceptions. For example, in the case of a small church with very limited leadership potential, some changes in the types of positions might be required. But good reasons should underlie any departure from this proven and widely used principle of fitting men to the positions rather than fitting the positions to the men.

An Existing Organization

When we come to the problem of *reorganizing* an established institution, the approach should be modified. Gulick has stated:

> In any practical situation, the problem of organization must be approached from *both* top and bottom. This is particularly true in the reorganization of a going concern. May it not be that this practical necessity is likewise the sound process theoretically? In that case one would develop the plan of an organization or reorganization both from the top downward and from the bottom upward, and would reconcile the two at the center. In planning the first subdivisions under the chief executive, the principle of the limitation of the span of control must apply; in building up the first aggregates of specialized functions the principle of homogeneity must apply.[12]

Now only a great deal of familiarity with organizational problems will provide the insight for recognizing the wisdom of this dual approach to the problem of organization. But it should be evident to the reader that reorganization must involve an accurate knowledge of both the supervisory and leadership positions as well as the jobs to be supervised at all levels, or the very likely result will be tensions, misunderstandings, and in some cases, organizational collapse. If the dual approach is not used, an executive may find himself working with an unrealistic organizational structure in which there are a great many generals

[12] Institute of Public Administration, *Papers on the Science of Administration,* Edited by Luther Gulick and L. Urwick, pp. 11-12. Italics supplied.

and no privates or just the reverse. Quite obviously, the ideal is to have a proper balance between the two groups. Both leaders and workers are needed for an organization to be successful.

Span of Control

As one thinks about the organization or reorganization of a church institution, he should be aware of the organizational principle called the *span of control*. From the standpoint of administration in our public schools, we find:

> The term "span of control" has come into the literature of business and civil administration. It means that *for effective administration there is a limit to the number of individuals from whom the top administrator may personally receive reports and with whom he may discuss and determine programs of action.*[13]

The observation of this principle is important also for the minister-administrator in either the small or large church. For as soon as a man begins to work directly with a large number of persons he reduces his effectiveness. All other factors being equal, it is far easier to work with three persons than with twenty. This is due to the fact that there are many less relationships in the former situation than in the latter. Greicunas has computed the number of relationships that result as the number of subordinates increases.

> In almost every case the supervisor measures the burden of his responsibility by the number of direct single relationships between himself and those he supervises. But in addition there are direct group relationships and cross relationships. Thus if Tom supervises two persons, Dick and Harry, he can speak to them individually, or he can speak to them as a pair. The behavior of Dick in the presence of Harry or of Harry in the presence of Dick will vary from their behavior when with Tom alone. Further, what Dick thinks of Harry and what Harry thinks of Dick constitute two cross relationships which Tom must keep in mind in arranging any work over which they must collaborate in his absence. . . . Thus even in this extremely

[13] *The American School Superintendency,* Thirtieth Yearbook of the American Association of School Administrators, National Education Association, p. 69.

simple unit of organization, Tom must hold four to six relationships within his span of attention.[14]

Greicunas goes on to say (in reference to a man with four subordinates and contemplating a fifth):

> Just why an executive already having four subordinates should hesitate before adding a fifth member to the group which he controls directly, becomes clear if it is realized that the addition not only brings twenty new relationships with him, but adds nine more relationships to each of his colleagues. The total is raised from forty-four to a hundred possible relationships for the unit . . . an increase in complexity of one hundred twenty-seven percent in return for a 20 percent increase in working capacity.[15]

Greicunas then proceeds to show how the total direct and cross relationships increase as new members are added to the span of control. For example, with five persons the number of relationships moves upward to 100. If ten persons are included in the span of control, the number of relationships rises to 5,210 (an impossible number of relationships to recognize and supervise adequately). And if the total of twelve persons is included in the span of control then the number of relationships is multiplied to 24,708![16]

Some of the *guides* to a manageable span of control are these: (a) the more complex the work of subordinates is, the narrower the span should be, i.e., the less the number of persons the span should include, (b) the more responsibility and authority a subordinate carries, the narrower the span should be. The underlying reasons for this approach to executive action are that complexity of work often involves the correlation of knowledge from many different fields, and the greater the responsibility one carries, the more he is faced with difficult problems, the solutions to which require a great deal of time with one's superiors for discussion and approval. If, however, superiors and executives operate with too wide a span of control, much of their time will be expended on relatively unimportant matters. The time of administrators should be devoted as much as possible to

14 Gulick and Urwick, *Papers on the Science of Administration*, p. 184.
15 *Ibid.*, p. 185.
16 *Ibid.*, p. 186.

matters of great import and of special significance. Items of lesser importance should be treated by men on the lower levels of the organization.

Summary

The organization of an enterprise is by no means a simple task. Because of this, it often engages the attention of church leaders to the point where it becomes an end rather than a means, where it becomes all-important and submerges the individuality of its participating members. We must ever remember that:

> Organization is the vehicle which carries the program toward its goal. It provides the machinery for cooperative effort on the part of persons. It is not itself the goal, but is the means of achieving the goal. Organization in the church exists for the sake of the Christian religion, not for its own sake. Whenever it becomes an end in itself, it no longer justifies its existence.[17]

In so far as the above concept prevails in the churches, the following summary principles of organization should be of significant assistance:

(1) The purpose of organization is to secure the accomplishment of institutional objectives, especially its unique and primary objective.

(2) Although organizational charts have their limitations, their advantages sufficiently outweigh their disadvantages to make them eminently worthwhile.

(3) An effective organization provides for both a line and a staff, with unity of management present in the line to as great a degree as possible. The functions of the line and staff should be clear to all persons in the organization. The function of the line, as we have indicated, is to direct activities and make decisions; the function of the staff is to advise.

(4) The wise administrator will recognize the existence of informal groups or cliques and attempt to integrate them constructively into the formal organization.

---

[17] Division of Christian Education, *The Organization and Administration of Christian Education in the Local Church,* National Council of the Churches of Christ in the United States of America, p. 27.

(5) Generally speaking, new organizations are organized from the top down. Older organizations are organized (or reorganized) from both the top and the bottom simultaneously.

(6) The number of persons supervised by an executive in the line depends upon several factors, among which are: (a) the variety of tasks performed by the subordinates, (b) the degree of responsibility connected with the tasks performed by subordinates. Usually, the span of control becomes smaller the higher one moves in an organization.

After a group has identified its primary objective, i.e., its reason for existence, and has arranged its members in appropriate vertical and horizontal relationships so that it has, in effect, become an organization, it is then ready to consider its program of planning — a subject which is discussed at length in the following chapter.

References to Administrative Techniques in Appendix

1. Note the organizational aspects of administrative Technique 12.

2. Study Technique 13 for the elements involved in establishing a new program.

III

Planning

Anyone acquainted with the business world is aware of the fact that no business enterprise can attempt to manufacture everything from toys to missiles. There are choices which must be made. He also knows that there are few universities today, if any, that attempt to train men at the highest level in all subject areas. Some universities are noted for their specialization in the fields of law, science, and medicine, but it can be safely said that no university in our present day specializes in *every* field.

Just as it is necessary for commercial enterprises and schools to make choices and set up realistic objectives, even so must churches do the same. We believe that the church has at least one unique goal which is exclusively its own. It is unreservedly committed to the objective of communicating the gospel of reconciliation to lost men. And moreover it is committed to a program designed to train and to educate the spiritual dimension of man's personality as he is related to God through faith in Christ Jesus our Lord. The selection and careful definition of specific objectives is the next step in the process. Planning cannot be conducted effectively without clearly defined goals. But once the goals have been chosen and stated, then the subsequent steps in the planning process can be taken.

Planning Defined

Planning is the process of examining the past and the present in order to construct the best program for achieving the church's objectives in both present and future. From this definition it is obvious that the planning that we do is not an end of the administrative process but simply a means to an end. Listen to what Sears has to say in his volume *The Nature of the Administrative Process*:

> Though planning can and often must be carried on as a separate function, it is never in itself a final end, but always a means to an end. As such, it becomes a first step in something beyond itself. This something may be further planning; but ultimately the planning is completed and its product is ready for use. The use of planning is to discover and prepare the way for some needed decision or some action to be taken.[1]

The ever-present need, of course, is to forecast as accurately as possible the circumstances which will exist in the future and then plan one's program in the light of such knowledge. Forecasting is not an easy undertaking but it must be done if goals and objectives are to be effectively achieved. This requires the collection and the interpretation of relevant data from past programs (both successful and unsuccessful) and also from present ones, so that judgments of a dependable nature can be made for future action. Planning, therefore, studies the past and the present, gathers data, interprets these, and then makes plans for the future with the ultimate end in mind of achieving the organization's established goals.

Importance of Planning

Why do we feel that the planning process is so very important? Because without planning, a church's objectives will be only partially achieved, if at all. A lack of proper planning likewise produces a program which is characterized by haphazard "last minute," "emergency" meetings and activities, frequently dictated by cliques or pressure groups.

---

[1] Jesse B. Sears, *Nature of the Administrative Process*, pp. 40-41.

Since time and energy will be expended along with a financial investment of either large or small degree, only the most acceptable program should be developed. We must not squander the resources which God has given but use them wisely in the preparation of our church's educational programs. In what way can this best be done?

Blackwood suggests that a church desiring to economize with regard to time and effort should arrange for a planning conference each fall. In this way a church will be a careful steward of the time and energy of its members.

> In the autumn many a pastor arranges for a planning conference. Or rather he works with the officers in making such arrangements. At a quiet spot remote from the sanctuary the officers and other leaders spend an afternoon and evening thinking and praying about the strategy and tactics. They need not employ these terms, but somehow they consider the need for objectives and plans for reaching them. . . . When the planning conference adjourns, everyone ought to know why the home church exists, and what it hopes to accomplish this next year. How else can the congregation expect to do its part in winning the warfare against sin?[2]

Planning is an essential factor in the work and life of the church today perhaps more than ever before. It is important for the implementation of the visitation program, for working out the attendance increase efforts, and for the evangelistic outreach. Social and fellowship activities also require careful planning if they are to be a genuine contribution to the life of the participants. Fellowship programs which are not planned carefully will soon fail to be of interest to those outside the church and may not be too highly successful in creating interest among those within it.

Planning, however, can become an administrative fetish. As a consequence it may be carried too far into the future and with too great a measure of specificity, so that with changing circumstances, necessary modifications become extremely difficult to make. But if there is to be an effective, comprehensive program operating within the church, it certainly must proceed on a

[2] Andrew W. Blackwood, *Pastoral Leadership*, p. 16.

foundation of some type of realistic planning. To neglect planning is but to jeopardize the work of Christ in the church.

Function of Planning

The specific function of planning is that of establishing goals and indicating the means for their achievement. In point of time or sequence, planning is the process which lays out the program that is to be implemented at a future date. It is basically the predictive element that characterizes the function of planning. This is the ability to forecast the circumstances that will prevail in the future and then to prepare the program that will be the most appropriate in attaining the organization's objectives.

Objectives

The church leader soon discovers that objectives should exist at every organizational level — objectives unique to the levels themselves but which harmonize with and lead toward, and into, the more general objectives located on the highest levels. Since the selection and formulation of objectives are part of the planning process, it follows that planning as well as objectives will be found at every organizational level within an institution, be it a church, a school, or a business enterprise. Because of this, a hierarchy of objectives exists in every successful organization (see Figure 6). In our Sunday church schools, for example, there are specific class objectives which lead into the broader and more inclusive departmental objectives. The departmental objectives will in turn lead into and assist in the achievement of the Sunday church school objectives. Beyond this we find that the objectives of the Sunday church school focus upon and lead into the very general and therefore some of the broadest of all objectives — those of the church itself. The goals of a particular church aim at denominational or interdenominational objectives, and these ultimately at the one all-inclusive objective of loving the God who first loved us.

Consideration should also be given to objectives in terms of time as well as in terms of their relationship to the organizational

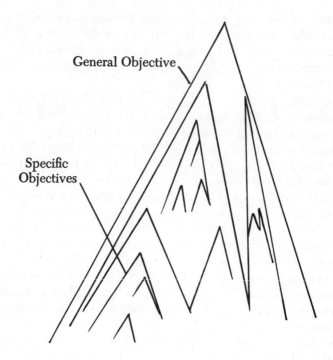

Graphic Illustration of Relationship between
General and Specific Objectives

Figure 6

This diagram is adapted from one by H. H. Remmers and H. L. Gage in their *Educational Measurement and Evaluation*, Revised Edition, Harper and Brothers, N.Y., 1955, p. 32.

structure. Some objectives can be reached rather quickly whereas others require much longer. Those which call for an extended period of time for their attainment are known as long-range objectives and those requiring a lesser period as short-range objectives.

Long-Range Objectives. This type of objective projects into the future for many months and often for years. There seems to be no concensus as to the definition of "long-range" but it would appear that objectives and plans which extend beyond a year may be given this classification. Such objectives should be tentative in nature so that with a possible shift in circumstances, changes can be made easily. Long-range objectives with their accompanying long-range plans should be designed in outline form — not in great detail. For, if greatly detailed explanations and specifications are set down and then at a later date major modifications must be made, the details will be difficult to change and much of the time invested in the detailed planning will be lost. Thus, it is far better to fill in gradually the details of long-range plans as the time for their implementation approaches.

Short-Range Objectives. Objectives of this type may be described as those which are to be attained in a year or less. If in the month of September, for example, a large adult Sunday church school department sets up a goal of visiting its entire membership during the following January, then most of the details of the program will undoubtedly be in final form by the first of December. The general principle involved is this: the less time there is available for the achievement of an objective or the less time there is before a plan is to be initiated, the greater must be the specificity of detail in the early stages of planning.

Calendars

One example of advanced planning is that involving the use of church calendars. There are of course many types of planning calendars. But two of the most important ones are known as the Activities Calendar and the Advanced Information or Promotion Calendar. On the Activities Calendar are placed those

PROPOSED PROGRAM AND ESTIMATE OF FUNDS NEEDED FOR IT

	Check Appropriate Column		Estimated Cost
	We Recommend for the New Year	Our Long Range Dreams	

1. Winning Pupils to Christ and the Church (Manual pages 30, 31)

Any recommendations from leader or committee in this area? Yes ☐ No ☐

Annual meeting of the Commission on Education with the Commission on Membership and Evangelism present to plan the details of the year's church school evangelistic program.

An annual school of evangelistic teaching.

Teachers and leaders informed and encouraged in their responsibility as personal evangelists.

Distribution and use of Teacher's Responsibility List.

Ordering and use of church school evangelistic literature.

Full use of the Easter season in church school evangelism.

2. Recruiting and Training Leaders (Manual pages 32, 33)

Any recommendations from leader or committee in this area? Yes ☐ No ☐

Discovery and enlistment of needed teachers and workers.

Local church leadership training program.

City, subdistrict or district training program.

Sending leaders to conference and other training centers.

Encouraging youth and young adults to enter church vocations.

3. Lesson Materials and Teaching Procedures (Manual pages 34, 35)

Any recommendations from leader or committee in this area? Yes ☐ No ☐

Adequate provision for space for classes and groups.

Adequate lesson and other material for all classes and groups.

Leaflets, manuals and periodicals for all teachers and leaders.

Classroom supplies (paper, paste, crayon, etc.).

Classroom equipment (furniture, chalkboards, etc.).

Audio-visual equipment (projectors, speakers, etc.).

Purchase and rental of audio-visuals (films, records, slides, etc.).

Books for the church school library.

4. Increasing Membership and Attendance (Manual pages 40, 41)

Any recommendations from leader or committee in this area? Yes □ No □

An active membership cultivation superintendent (*Discipline*, par. 143.8).
An understanding throughout the church of the importance of increasing church school membership and attendance.
Membership workers supplied with guidance literature.
Membership rolls and attendance records adequately maintained.
A continual search for prospective new members, with adequate follow-up.
Annual presentation to the commission by the membership cultivation superintendent of comprehensive plan for membership and attendance increase throughout the whole church school.

5. Christian Stewardship and Giving (Manual pages 42, 43)

Any recommendations from leader or committee in this area? Yes □ No □

All pupils taught the principles of Christian stewardship involving Christian use of money and support of the church and other worthy causes.
Tithing emphasized as a minimum plan of proportionate giving.
An annual budget for the church school.
Adequate money handling procedures through the church school.
Promotion of personal giving to church budget and related causes.
Promotion and observance each fourth Sunday of World Service Sunday in the church school.
Annual observance of Church School Rally Day with offering.
Promotion of Methodist Youth Fund.
Promotion of Children's Service Fund.

6. Missionary Education (Manual pages 44, 45)

Any recommendations from leader or committee in this area? Yes □ No □

Co-operative plans being followed for missionary education of children and youth.
Adequate use of mission study units, with particular reference to adults.
Special missionary programs in Methodist Sunday Evening Fellowship and as appropriate throughout the church school.
Co-operation with Commission on Missions in annual church-wide school of missions.
Encouragement of adequate and systematic giving to missions.

Money total ....

Figure 7. Short-Range and Long-Range Planning Form.
Source: "Program Builder Worksheet," Methodist Church, p. 2.

events, programs, and projects for an entire quarter (or preferably for a year) with the activities near at hand displaying essential information. Events listed on this calendar should give answers to the questions: *Who* is involved? *Where* will the event take place or be held? *When* will it occur? *How* will it be arranged? *What* is its major purpose?

The Advanced Information or Promotion Calendar is designed to operate *in advance* of the Activities Calendar. It has two general purposes: (1) it presents information about the time and place of an activity thereby facilitating the planning and coordination of other activities, and (2) it provides opportunity for making up announcements, brochures, and other materials for creating interest.

Cautions

There is always the danger that plans, once formulated, will not be implemented. Schleh has suggested the following method for preventing this condition from developing:

> One of the reasons for a lack of action was that the new-products committee was responsible for carrying through on sub-goals. This procedure is often the source of "no action" on a problem. It is harder to get action if a committee takes the responsibility for meeting goals. An individual can usually best achieve a sub-goal. One way for a chief executive to get action is to insist that all sub-goals, at least, are assigned to "a man."[3]

Along with the assignment of sub-goals to individuals, Schleh also recommends putting a plan into operation even though some of the details are not perfectly complete:

> One of the shackles to action that binds many companies is the assumption that everything has to be perfect. Some men feel that a plan must be absolutely right before any action is taken.
>
> Instead, simply make sure that the *general* plan is sound. Assuming that details can be changed as the procedure gets under way, gets action started much sooner. In actual practice, minor changes can usually be made without much trouble. If the general plan is sound and the sub-plans have been laid out, minor defects in them can be corrected as the program is put in.[4]

[3] Edward C. Schleh, *Successful Executive Action*, p. 10.
[4] *Ibid.*, pp. 10-11.

Another caution to be observed involves the assignment, by an administrator, of goals which appear to the individual to be unattainable. If an administrator sets up overly ambitious objectives, his subordinates may be so overwhelmed by the scope of the objectives that they panic or develop an emotional block. The administrator, therefore, must learn to assign only those goals which are possible of achievement and are realistic in the eyes of those who will be carrying the major part of the load.

Levels of Planning

In addition to formulating objectives and designing plans, the administrator will soon discover that there are a great many decisions which must be made in the execution of plans. It has been said that a good plan poorly executed may be less effective than a poor plan that is well executed. If all of the decisions involved in the execution of a plan could be made at the highest level of an organization, where the most capable persons are to be found, perhaps inefficiency could be greatly reduced. Unfortunately, however, decisions must be made at every level of the organization, beginning at the highest and proceeding to the lowest level.

The rules which help to guide the decision-making process at all levels are generally known as the policies of an institution. Policies are relatively permanent in nature and are designed to be broad in their application. They assist in the execution of an organization's plans and help to govern different persons and operations located at levels either identical with or below the level at which the policy-making occurs.

Policy-Making and Planning

It should be noted that "policy" as an administrative term is used in different ways. Simon, in his *Administrative Behavior*, discusses the use of this term by other writers when he says that "policy" may be (a) the general rule laid down by superiors working at many organizational levels to limit the unrestricted use of individual judgment by their subordinates in regard to administrative procedures or (b) the more important rules set down by *top management*.[5] Newman also discusses the use of the term "policy" and eventually subsumes it under the concept of "standing plans":

> Standing plans, which are used over and over again include policies, organization structure, standard procedures, and standard methods.[6]

In any case, policies are general principles of operation which provide guidance, stability, and consistency for an organization.

The value of policies lies in their expeditious nature. If the policy-making function has been active and carefully guided, most of the hundreds of decisions connected with planning which must be made week after week and month after month can be made at the level where problems arise and where the decisions for solving such problems will be implemented. Without a comprehensive set of policies to guide them, however, men at the lower organizational levels would be required to submit all questions and problems to those at the top levels — to those who probably are already overburdened with more tasks and decisions to make than time allows them to deal with adequately.

Policies are also valuable for lending stability to an organization. When decisons are made, not on the basis of whim or caprice, but on the basis of principle, people come to realize that there is consistency within an organization and that the solutions to problems are not the result of arbitrary and impulsive thinking. Favoritism is more likely to be frowned upon, and a greater measure of justice, of understanding, and of fairness in the decision-making process will be present if general policies are part of an organization's planning program. The only al-

---

[5] Herbert A. Simon, *Adminstrative Behavior*, p. 59. If the reader is interested in pursuing the philosophical and psychological aspects of policy-making and decision-making, he should read Chaps. 4 and 5 of Simon's volume. He points up the confusion in the use of terminology in administrative circles today and helps to clear away some of the obscurities.

[6] Newman, *Administrative Action*, p. 53. Although Newman makes an attempt earlier in his volume (p. 46) to distinguish between these elements, he admits that many of the terms are used "interchangeably" in the business world.

ternative to administration through policies is administration through arbitrariness and capriciousness.

Policy-Making and Implementation

Policy-making as we have indicated should not be confined to the highest level of an organization. It should be found at *every* level. Some of the levels in the church at which policy-making will occur are the following:

Level I — Board Level. In many churches, e.g., the Baptist and the Congregational, the highest policy-making body in theory is the congregation, but in administrative practice it frequently becomes the boards which are elected by the church to carry out its business (except in quarterly or annual meetings). The highest governing body of a church, therefore, regardless of the type of church government followed, carries a great degree of responsibility and authority. It may be known as the Session, as the Official Board, or by some similar title. In any case, the policies which are laid down by the highest official group of a church are usually of a very general nature and influence the entire program of the church. As a matter of fact, the higher the organizational level at which a group is located, the more general the policies will be with which they will concern themselves. Since most policies formulated at board levels are employed for long periods of time and affect a great many people, they should be given careful consideration and should be formulated and put into operation only after they have been accurately phrased.

Level II — Church Staff.[7] This group is usually charged with the execution of plans and policies laid down by the Board of Education, by the Session, or by the Official Board. Policies, of course, may be executed by (a) committees, (b) the Church Staff, or (c) the Church Staff in cooperation with committees. The Minister of Christian Education, for example, is given the

---

[7] In churches with a congregational form of church government, the pastor may be placed on a level equal with the boards and subject only to the congregation in which case he would be placed on Level I rather than Level II. In practice, however, the pastor participates at both levels in that he usually participates in policy-making at the board level and in the execution of policies at the staff level.

task in most churches of sharing responsibility for the Christian education program of a church with committees and boards. However, depending upon the provisions in the church constitution, he may be given complete responsibility for directing the program without sharing responsibility with any group at his level.

Level III — Superintendents and Supervisors. This group comprises another level of administration and consists largely of supervisors, counselors, and superintendents. They are concerned with the best methods and techniques for executing the policies which have been formulated at both levels above them. In addition to these policies, however, the personnel at this level may also formulate policies which will be of lesser importance than those established at higher levels but nonetheless essential to operations at this level and those below. Whatever policies are drawn up at this level must be in common agreement with the policies formed at other levels if conflict is to be avoided and a coherent, unified program is to result.

Level IV — Teachers, Workers, and Members. This is the level at which most plans are finally implemented. There is always the danger that a plan will be incorrectly implemented or will completely fail at this point. However, if the planning process has been carried out according to good administrative practice, little difficulty should be experienced. Important to the implementation of the plans is the understanding and the good will of those who operate at this level. If they are acquainted with the details, if they understand the purpose, and if they have been invited to sit in on the early stages of the planning process, they will usually cooperate and put the plans into effective operation. But it is a well-known maxim in the field of administration that *those things which workers and subordinates do not understand they will suspect and most reluctantly (if at all) put into operation.* What they have not been informed of, in other words, they will both suspect and in many cases actively oppose.

A reluctance to implement plans may be found in either church or secular situations. In the case of secular organizations, the economic factor is frequently employed to bring about cooperation for the implementation of plans. There is no such economic incentive for members in a church. Instead it must be a matter of loyalty to God and to the church which motivates them to carry out the plans which have been developed. Certainly the church cannot and should not rely on threats and intimidations for the implementation of plans as the secular world has so often done, but rather it must teach and practice the principles of Christian love and concern for all men. Only in this way can the program of Christ be effectively planned, directed, and carried forward.

Pattern of Planning

For the person who is inexperienced in administration, there is a general pattern of planning with which he should be familiar. That is, there are certain stages or steps involved in all good planning. Sometimes an executive moves so quickly over several stages that it seems he is "skipping" parts of the planning process, but upon close examination it will be found that he has gone through each stage either at a conscious or subconscious level.

(1) *Defining the Problem.* The first step in planning involves the isolation and careful delineation of the problem that confronts a group. The question must be asked, "What is the *exact* nature of this problem?" And, "Do we have more than one problem here?" One method for assuring that the problem has been properly outlined and defined is to cast it into the form of a *short, simple sentence or phrase.* This is not to be taken as a "foolproof" method for defining a problem, but it does help to avoid drawing in additional problems through the use of the extra clauses and phrases of compound and complex sentences.

From the standpoint of administrative planning, the solution to a recognized and well-defined problem may become an objective toward which a program moves. If the problem of juvenile delinquency, for example, exists in a church community, this becomes a problem for the church as well. If a decision is made by the church to make a major effort toward solving this problem, then the solution which is sought becomes one of the church's objectives. It might select as an objective the following:

61

"To Set Up a Church-Sponsored Weekday Youth Program as a Means of Helping the Community Combat Juvenile Delinquency." Hence the suggested solution to a problem may become an objective for an organization, be it a church, a school, or other institution in our society.

(2) *Suggesting Possible Solutions.* Our problem may be one of combating juvenile delinquency. It may be that of choosing between the relocation of a church or the expansion of its present facilities. Whatever the nature of the problem, once it has been defined, the next step is that of setting down several specific solutions. That there could easily be several solutions connected with the above problems should of course be evident. It becomes the responsibility of the group or the administrator to select the one plan which seems most plausible in the light of the experience, background, and resources of the group. One general rule in this regard is that the larger the problem, the more comprehensive the plan will be that is required for its solution, and the more likely it will be that the group considering the plans be composed of members representing the various phases of the church's program. Why should this be? Because major problems influence for good or for ill many areas of a church program, and the people who work in such areas logically want to be represented on those groups that make plans which will ultimately affect them. Furthermore, some persons will make contributions based upon their wealth of experience and intimate relationship over the years with the church and its program. There will undoubtedly be others who will devote a portion of their time to the creation of new ideas and suggestions and place them at the disposal of those in the planning group. Even those who desire to register complaints and criticism may contribute valuable assistance and should not be ignored. Directly related material from *all* sources and persons should be sought and carefully considered.

(3) *Gathering Relevant Data.* It is not enough to choose the specific solution or plan that *seems* to be the most satisfactory. Rather, we must collect as much data as possible in order to confirm or reject the selection we have made. An effort should be made to list all the data which will be necessary for verifying the selection. For example, if it is a choice between relocating

or expanding the present facilities of a church, perhaps a community census should be taken. What is the population turnover of the community? To what extent will the area be industrialized five years hence? How many people have come into the community in the last ten years? And how many have left in the same period? What is the ethnic population in this area? What kinds of transportation facilities are available? All of these questions and many others should be considered in this step. One may also compose a questionnaire and distribute it to the church membership and to those in the community, depending, of course, upon the nature of the information sought. Arrangements may be made also for personal interviews with leading citizens in order to discover what their predictions are about the future of the area in which the church is located. Surveys conducted by the federal, state, or city governments should not be overlooked in the search for factual material.

Once the data have been collected, they should be assembled and put into the form of tables and graphs so that they may be interpreted easily. For in the final analysis it is the *interpretation* of the facts which will guide in all decision-making and will ultimately determine the plan to be selected.

(4) *Forecasting the Future.* Forecasting is to some extent implied in the previous step, yet it means not only looking at plans which seem to be the most desirable for the present, but also at plans which seem to be the most desirable for the future. What will things be like not only five but ten and fifteen years from now? Certainly this question must be answered as accurately as possible from the data which are gathered if planning is to be intelligently done.

(5) *Making the Decision.* There are those who say that this step should not be a difficult one if all of the previous steps have been followed through carefully. Simon disagrees with this view, however. He clearly stipulates that decision-making is extremely difficult in that it takes place within an environment involving both psychological and sociological factors. He says that the particular factors to be found in the environment tend to influence the decision-making process to a very considerable degree.

> The deliberate control of the environment of decision permits not only the integration of choice, but its socialization as well. Social institutions may be viewed as regularizations of the behavior of individuals through subjection of their behavior to stimulus-patterns socially imposed on them. It is in these patterns that an understanding of the meaning and function of organization is to be found.[8]

Simon means by this, that when the members of an institution can anticipate the behavior of others through knowing their purposes, motives, interests, and values, they can meet and more rationally consider the data and the decisions which ought to be made. Most administrators will agree that the weightier the decisions to be made and the more people there will be affected by a decision, the greater should be the time available for gathering data of all types, including the psychological and sociological. If, on the other hand, it is a decision which will affect a limited number of persons and will not exert much influence upon their lives, then comparatively less time is needed for gathering facts and reaching decisions.

(6) *Preparing the Plans.* An outgrowth of the decision-making process is the choice of objectives, the means for implementing them, and an outline of points at which evaluation should occur. In other words, comprehensive plans are prepared in more or less detail.

The objectives stated in the plans are a reflection of the decisions which have been made about the areas in which the church expects to serve. Few pastors and churches can expect to minister effectively in all directions and in all areas. Choices must be made. Some pastors and churches focus on a great pulpit ministry, some on a counseling ministry, others on a teaching ministry, and still others on a ministry of evangelism or a combination of several of these.

Again, resource leaders from every facet of church life will be brought in to consider the plans and make suggestions. Questions which will have significance are: Who will give direction to the plan? What equipment and supplies will be necessary? Which activities should receive immediate attention? How much financial assistance is needed initially? Are there any

---

[8] Simon, *op. cit.*, p. 109.

operations which should receive top priority throughout the execution period of the plans? And at what points should the progress of the work be checked and evaluated (and by what means)? All of these questions and many more must be asked in this stage of planning.

(7) *Acceptance of the Plans.* This must be done by the proper board or group. In most churches, plans of direct concern to the entire membership are voted upon at an official church business meeting. This is not only proper but in the best interests of the church since the necessary funds for the implementation of plans come ultimately from the congregation. Plans with limited application, of course, will be voted upon by the groups primarily concerned with their operation.

(8) *Securing the Funds and Personnel.* The final step deals with the securing of financial support and appropriate leadership. Effective fund-raising and the selection of leadership provide the basis for the implementation of a church's plans. Each church, however, must solve its financial and leadership problems in its own way. Churches which find themselves in similar but perhaps not identical circumstances may use the same methods with relative success. But a church must be cautious about adopting the techniques of other churches. A church is an *institutional personality* and administrators become keenly aware of this fact, especially when they begin a fund drive. No two churches are alike, and the methods used for raising funds and securing leadership will vary from church to church. Nevertheless, if the previous steps in the planning process have been thoroughly and carefully taken, this final step should be a successful and satisfactory one for all concerned.

Factors Conditioning Planning

Is it possible for a church executive to spend more time in planning than the fruits of such planning will warrant? When can we say that excessive planning has occurred? Of course, there is no set rule for determining the answers to such questions, but the suggestions which follow may be helpful.

When one begins to spend more time in planning an event than the event itself will take, he should question whether the event is worth all the time that is involved. This does not imply that he should refuse to invest more time in planning than the event will take. Nevertheless he should be certain that the event is an extremely important one if twice as much time or more is consumed in planning as the event itself will require. The delivery of a sermon, however, is an activity approximately thirty minutes in length, yet requiring from 12 to 25 hours for preparation — and rightly so. But if this much time were devoted by a pastor to planning the athletic activities at an annual church picnic, he might well raise serious questions about the value received from the time invested.

One should also question whether a great deal of time should be invested if the plans could be easily remembered and are to be used but a single time. It is understandable why one might carry out planning in great detail and put down each specification if such a plan is to be used annually or at least periodically. If the plan is to be used but once, however, the administrator has a responsibility to ask whether the time to be used is justified.

There is the further question of whether the plans will be revised or modified at a later date. If there is such a possibility, then many hours of planning, especially at the level of detail, would not be justified and one would do well to simply map out the general points, make up an outline of the plans, and put the details in as they are needed.

Finally, if a plan is less important than other plans or activities, one would do well to delegate the details of the plan to an aide or set such a plan to one side and be satisfied with a brief sketch of the main points.

The Administrator's Part in Planning

Whether an administrator likes it or not he is ultimately held responsible for the success or failure of all plans. This is particularly true for the pastor of a church. Someone else may have been in complete charge of a program that collapsed, but *he*, the minister, will be the one to suffer the consequences in the long run, since he is the chief leader in the church, and the congregation (and sometimes even the community) will hold him responsibile for any major failures in the organization. He must therefore take time to plan.

A Personal Schedule

The importance of planning one's own personal schedule is self-evident. For one thing, it will call attention to the fact that

WORK DISTRIBUTION CHART				
Name: Rev. Mr. John Smith		Position: Pastor		
Rat-ing	Description of Operation		No. Items	Hrs. W'kly
1	Sermon Preparation			
2	Teaching Responsibilities			
3	Special Services: Weddings, Funerals, etc.			
4	Pastoral Visitation			
5	Counseling			
6	Office Correspondence			
7	Attending Meetings and Conferences			
8	Answering Telephone			
9	Miscellaneous (Filing, Planning Own Work, etc.)			
	Total Hours Work			
Date:				

Figure 8

Weekly Work Distribution Chart for Determining Work Load and Importance of Job Operations.

a certain part of the week should be devoted to planning activities. If an administrator puts into writing his chief duties and plans, it will be possible to identify any that may have been neglected or overlooked. Moreover, if he will list his responsibilities and provide time for them in his schedule, he can quickly determine that point at which he must make time adjustments. Scheduling all duties on a chart will also enable him to select at a future date the activities which are of lesser importance and thereby take the necessary steps for assigning these to others. Without a schedule, however, the administrator of a growing church becomes more and more frustrated, not knowing why so little time is available to him and not knowing which of his many duties could be legitimately and properly delegated to other personnel. (See Figure 8 for an example of a work distribution chart.)

Three Types of Planning

From time to time a situation will arise demanding that all activities be dropped and every available resource be focused upon the problem at hand. If there is a threat to the safety and welfare of a group, quick action is needed. To delay may mean a loss of life. A fire, a storm, or an undiagnosed illness may bring tragedy and deep sorrow if plans are not immediately set up and made operational. Of course, the number of such situations may be reduced if previous planning has been done. And this is the ideal way. Standing or ready-made plans should be in the hands of leaders so that when an emergency arises they will know what steps to take. It should be remembered that emergencies may arise not only on church property, but also at church-sponsored activities which are held at homes, beaches, picnic grounds, camps, lakes, etc. No one, obviously, can foresee all of the possible emergency situations. When the unexpected and urgent situation arises, immediate emergency planning will be called for by the pastor or other administrator.

Another type of planning which the administrator must do involves the new and unusual, such as an unexpected need for additional equipment, expanding church facilities, or hiring new personnel. Though situations of this nature are not of the "emergency" type, they demand planning which falls between the routine and the urgent. If the administrator's schedule is somewhat flexible, he will be able to adjust his program so that for a limited period of time many of his energies can be directed toward the solution of the unique problems which confront him. If he fails to give sufficiently prompt and adequate attention to the new and unusual situations which appear, he may find that these have moved from this category into the emergency category — a condition to be avoided if at all possible.

Routine planning is familiar to everyone but studied carefully by very few. Setting up a daily and weekly work load is part of this operation. Generally, a planning session is scheduled at the beginning of a week to outline the activities for that period, and sometimes, in addition, several minutes at the first of each day are used to make final arrangements for the work of that day.

Beyond the daily and weekly work load are those common duties which go on year in and year out: typing, filing, classifying, recording, and mailing. In order to minimize the weekly and daily routine planning, work-distribution plans should be prepared by all concerned. These are plans which list the duties for each staff member and give the approximate number of minutes of each day and each week devoted to such duties. If the hours of work per week total less than forty (or whatever the understood number of hours per week happens to be) then additional work is usually assigned. It should also be pointed out that work-distribution plans, when properly designed and used, relieve the administrator of the burden of "finding something for the staff to do." He *knows* that they have sufficient work to keep them occupied without overburdening them.[9]

Motivating Personnel

It is not always the easiest matter to get plans implemented. However, if the administrator will follow three suggestions, he may obtain more satisfactory results.

First, he should not insist that plans be perfect in every detail before they are put into operation.[10] Some matters can be

[9] See Fig. 8, p. 67 for an example of a work distribution form.
[10] *See Infra,* p. 56.

worked out as the plan moves through its successive stages. To insist on perfect plans is virtually to condemn any action for getting plans started while people are still interested and motivated. Second, those charged with carrying out the plans should have the opportunity of sitting with the administrator in a discussion session while he goes through the plan as a "dry run." This may be done by discussing each step of the plan and by possibly going through the motions of activities connected with the plan, to see if there are any remaining and unsolved problems. Going through the plan in this way helps others to visualize the plan's operation realistically. Finally, the administrator should make it clear that if difficulties are encountered in any stage of the plan, he is available for assistance and consultation.

Ultimate Responsibility

In the event that the pastor or minister of Christian education cannot approve plans which are drawn up by a board or other official group, what should he do? Certainly an administrator realizes that he will be required to assume final responsibility for the failure of any plan. He should therefore make his ideas and reasons known to the planning group if he feels that certain modifications suggested by him would make the plan a successful one. But if he is convinced that the plan suggested by the group is unwise, he may in a spirit of Christian love and understanding put his objections into writing, yet, as administrator, consent to fully implement the plan to the best of his ability. If the plan is successful the administrator has learned that not all wisdom and knowledge reside with him alone; if it fails he may always refer to the letter outlining his objections and thereby absolve himself to a limited extent. The only other alternative is to offer one's resignation, but this is not always necessary or desirable.

Summary

No institution can undertake to do everything. Choices must be made. In the case of a church, factors playing an important part in the selection of its goals will be theological, social, psychological, and geographical in nature. The planning process will, of course, reflect the goals and objectives which have been selected and will determine the type of program the church is to follow. Several of the principles of planning which have been discussed in this chapter are:

1. The Principle of Objectives. If an organization is going to be effective, objectives of two types should exist: (a) long-range objectives which are the basis for long-range plans, and (b) short-range objectives which are the basis for short-range plans (i.e., those to be fulfilled in less than a year).

2. The Principle of Investigation. Plans should be based on facts and trends in so far as research personnel and facilities permit.

3. Principle of Continuity. Good planning considers not only the past and present condition of an organization but also attempts to predict and prepare for the future so that coherence and unity characterize the program.

4. Principle of Flexibility. Plans should be sufficiently flexible so that modifications may be made without any serious loss of time and effort.

5. Principle of Policy-Making. The most important aspect of planning is policy-making. This should occur at all levels of an organization, but primarily at the highest levels.

6. Principle of Responsibility. After an administrator has approved a set of plans, he is responsible for both their successes and their failures. He cannot, and should not, accept responsibility for successful projects if he refuses to accept responsibility for projects which are unsuccessful.

References to Administrative Techniques in Appendix

1. Planning permeates practically all administrative activity and therefore employs most of the techniques listed in the Appendix. However, study the short- and long-range aspects of the following in particular: 1, 4, 6, 8, 10, 14, 16 and 17.
2. In respect to the above techniques, observe the extent to which planning reaches into the different areas of Christian education.

IV

Delegation in Administration

Introduction

As a minister thinks about the organizational structure of a church, he cannot but reflect on the responsibilities of the personnel who will direct the Christian education program. "What will their duties and responsibilities be?" he may ask himself. There is need, of course, to avoid duplication of effort. There is further need to distribute the work load so that those leading the organization are not charged with every activity ranging from policy-making to the purchase of paper clips.

It is possible, however, to ignore the principles of good administration and become so involved in the program of an organization that one commits two administrative sins: (1) exhausting oneself with work detail, and (2) depriving others in the Body of Christ from exercising their gifts and responsibilities in the ministry of the church. These administrative sins are not necessarily attributable to the lesser of God's servants. Note the experience, if you will, of Moses:

> . . . Moses sat to judge the people, and the people stood about Moses from morning till evening. When Moses' father-in-law saw all that he was doing for the people, he said, "What is this that you are doing for the people? Why do you sit alone, and all the people stand about you from morning till evening?" And Moses said to his father-in-law, "Because the people come to me to inquire of God; when they have a dispute, they come to me and I decide between a man and his neighbors, and I make them know the statutes of God and his decisions." Moses' father-in-law said to him, "What you are doing is not good. You and the

people with you will wear yourselves out, for the thing is too heavy for you; you are not able to perform it alone. Listen now to my voice; I will give you counsel, and God be with you! You shall represent the people before God, and bring their cases to God; and you shall teach them the statutes and the decisions, and make them know the way in which they must walk and what they must do. Moreover choose able men from all the people, such as fear God, men who are trustworthy and who hate a bribe; and place such men over the people as rulers of thousands, of hundreds, of fifties, and of tens. And let them judge the people at all times; every great matter they shall bring to you, but any small matter they shall decide themselves; so it will be easier for you, and they will bear the burden with you. If you do this, and God so commands you, then you will be able to endure, and all this people also will go to their place in peace." So Moses gave heed to the voice of his father-in-law and did all that he had said (Exod. 18:13-24).

Moses' initial administrative error is not uncommon even today. One minister was heard to say, "I am not interested in an associate. It is too much effort to find something for him to do." Since his church was rather large, and since it was quite evident to the membership that he had a great many responsibilities, it was obviously not a matter of finding work for an associate but of an inability to delegate. Unfortunately, he was of the conviction that he alone could carry his multiplied responsibilities, though he was clearly discharging them in a very inadequate way. An attitude of this nature can oftentimes lead one down the road to failure. Laird reports that in an analysis of some 500 leaders, it was found that 73 per cent were good or excellent leaders and 27 per cent were fair, poor, or bad leaders. "The good and excellent leaders were found to be the ones who made the most use of delegating. The failures were concentrated among those who never, seldom, or occasionally delegated."[1] Urwick, too, has stated unequivocally: "without delegation no organization can function effectively. Yet, lack of the courage to delegate properly and of knowledge how to do it, is one of the most general causes of failure in organization."[2]

So we see that delegation is a most important aspect of organi-

[1] Donald A. Laird, and Eleanor C. Laird, *The Techniques of Delegating*, p. 43.
[2] Urwick, *Elements of Administration*, p. 51.

zation and administration. It is a process which cannot be ignored but rather should be recognized and employed intelligently by every church executive.

Importance of Delegation

Whether a church is large or small, delegation of some nature will be evident. It may be haphazard, it may be unsystematic, but it will be present. In so far as two or more persons are involved in carrying out a program, there will be a process of delegation, however limited it may be. Even in the simple social unit of the family, each member is responsible for certain common tasks. Delegation, in short, cannot be avoided in any organization regardless of size. The only question to be answered is whether it is to be done well or poorly. As Newman has indicated:

> Delegation takes place even in the smallest of administrative organizations. As soon as the plumber, the farmer, the manager of a corner grocery, or a real estate agent finds that he cannot perform all of the activities of his enterprise and hires an assistant, delegation takes place. In a large enterprise there are delegations not only from the president to the vice-presidents, but also redelegations by the vice-presidents to managers, managers to supervisors, and so on down the executive pyramid.[3]

The larger an organization becomes, the more important it is for an administrator to apply the principles of delegation. Those on the staff of a moderately large and growing church will of necessity concern themselves increasingly with more abstract operations, such as policy-making, supervision, counseling, and coordination. These more important activities can be adequately carried out, however, only if lesser important duties are delegated to Sunday-school superintendents, sponsors of youth groups, adult fellowship officers, and other leaders. As a matter of fact, the aim of the administrator ought to be that of utilizing the delegation process as frequently as possible so that duties and decisions of lesser significance will be transferred to those at the lower levels of the church structure. "The making of decisions," according to Pfiffner, "should ordinarily be delegated

---

[3] Newman, *Administrative Action*, p. 163.

to the lowest possible level of the hierarchy."[4] This will then permit him to devote himself to those administrative operations which demand the presence and skill of a full-time, well-trained staff person and will assure a continuing expansion of the church program.

The reasoning behind the general rule of delegating duties as far down the line as possible is that more time will be made available for working with purely administrative processes. Furthermore, the individual who is closest to the problems arising at the lower levels of an organization is oftentimes more qualified to make relevant decisions than are those on higher administrative levels. Why? Because he usually has a more intimate knowledge of the circumstances within which the problems have developed and out of which the solutions must come, if they are to come at all.

If those at each level of an organization are expected to accept delegated responsibilities, then it is vital for all who are connected with the program of the institution to receive appropriate training. For the training of personnel is the "life blood" of an organization. Without it, organization soon crumbles. However, delegation, as an educational process, can be employed for training personnel to accept responsibility and to make wise decisions. The more decisions and responsibilities there are delegated to subordinates, moreover, the greater will be their experience and the better prepared they will be for filling future leadership roles in the church and for rendering judgments on important organizational matters. Thus, delegation may have a twofold purpose: that of educating men in leadership skills, and that of freeing the administrator for more important activities.

What will it mean in a specific way for an organization if the administrator delegates? Will there be any increase in the effectiveness of the organization? Is it possible some persons will feel that the administrator who delegates is "shirking his duty?" The answers to these questions depend upon many factors. But, in general, it may be said that when people take responsibility, when they feel they are an integral part of the

---

[4] Pfiffner, *The Supervision of Personnel*, p. 51.

organization, they will take a greater interest in the program of the organization and, in addition, their morale will rise to a higher level simply because they feel that the organization is *their* organization. If the pastor maintains an accurate personal work schedule, moreover, it may later become the basis for: (1) identifying the responsibilities with the lowest priorities and delegating these, and (2) convincing the church that additional staff personnel are needed. Of course, if responsibilities are delegated indiscriminately, without due consideration of the abilities, time, and available energy of the persons involved, the load may be too heavy for them with a subsequent lowering of morale. Wisdom, understanding, and good judgment must be used in these matters as in all others.

Decisions Which May Be Delegated

The lesson which Moses learned was that of assigning the less important decisions and retaining for himself the more important ones. This implies that decisions and duties which are the least complex and require a lesser degree of skill and knowledge for their execution should be delegated to others. A further criterion which may be applied is: To what extent will the program be placed in jeopardy if an unwise decision should be made, or a responsibility not carried out? That is, how many people would be affected, and how seriously would the program of the church be damaged if "Jim Smith" failed to carry out his assigned responsibilities? To elaborate more fully upon the criteria for delegation, a delegator would do well to think about the following categories of decision-making for a delegatee:

(1) decisions of a routine nature

(2) decisions to be reported

(3) decisions requiring consultation[5]

Decisions of a Routine Nature

The first kind of decision one may be expected to delegate is that which is routine in nature and does not call for a report by

[5] By courtesy of *Fortune* Magazine, *The Executive Life*, pp. 137-138.

subordinates to their superiors. All decisions of this nature should be covered by written policies which are listed in a handbook or its equivalent, thus relieving a minister of many trivial decisions and unimportant problems. Decisions about such matters as the procurement of supplies, whom to call in the event of illness, where to obtain audio-visual aids, the reordering of staple materials, such as crayons, drawing paper, Sunday-school papers and curriculum materials are usually included in this category. That which has to do with the safety of church members should also be included in the handbook (so that one will find the welfare of the individual adequately provided for in the event of an accident). Matters of this and a similar nature should be included in the Christian education handbook of the church. If these subjects are incorporated into a manual, the vast majority of requests for assistance and supplies would not be funneled into the office of the church executive but would already be provided for. Without this type of printed aid, he would be literally swamped with details requiring more time than he would have available.

Decisions Followed by a Report

A second type of delegation is that which requires a report *after* the decision has been rendered and action taken. Thus the temporary appointment of a teacher by a department superintendent for a teaching assignment might be made until the Board of Christian Education has had opportunity to meet and give its approval. The purchase of *limited* supplies and equipment covered in a departmental budget may also be conducted without prior approval. If churches would operate as much as possible on the departmental level in respect to these and other similar matters, many of the decisions requiring immediate action could be made and reported at a later date to the Board, to receive the customary approval.

Decisions Requiring Consultation

A third type of delegation involves decisions which may be made *after consultation* with one's immediate superiors. This may or may not require the attention of persons at the top of the organizational structure depending on whether or not all concerned feel that the decision should be made by someone in the church office, namely, by one of the pastors or someone with the authority for making the decision at hand.

A department Sunday-school superintendent or youth sponsor, for example, may project a camping trip for his group. If, however, this activity is not covered in the printed instructions in the church handbook, he would feel an obligation to consult the Minister of Christian Education and secure his approval. We may say, then, that to plan a program, or to make any important decision not covered in the printed instructions, would be improper unless consultation and prior approval from one of the church staff or duly appointed authority had been obtained.

In view of the various types of decisions and duties which may be assigned, the administrator should use discretion in selecting the responsibilities to be delegated. It is especially important that personnel being inducted into an organization be apprised of their responsibilities and their duties as well as notified of decisions which they can make without consulting others. By the same token, they should be informed of decisions which should be made only after consulting and cooperating with specified persons or boards. As Sears has indicated:

> Positions should be clearly assigned, care being taken to relate the assignment to the objectives, organization . . . and program, as outlined in the rules; and with special explanations when discretionary power is to be delegated or when close cooperation with others will be involved. This can best be done at the time of appointment.[6]

Though one may find himself relatively successful in educating his delegatees, there will also be certain dangers connected with the delegation process.

Dangers Involved

Whenever an executive contemplates the delegation of responsibility, he must be prepared for criticism. This is simply due

[6] J. B. Sears, *Nature of the Administrative Process*, p. 305.

to the fact that some assignments will be inadequately performed by subordinates. More than this, if the duties which are delegated are not defined carefully and are not spelled out in detail, or if they are given out without due regard for the principle of unity of management, then the operation of the program may fail or be seriously affected. This is what Upson refers to when he says:

> Keep your lines of authority straight. Don't make somebody responsible for a job and give the same task or one in his bailiwick to his subordinate. The best way to wreck the morale of any organization is to pass out orders like campaign buttons regardless of who gets them, making privates believe that they are majors, and majors believe that they are nothing at all.[7]

In other words, delegation is similar to a scientific procedure in that careful handling and utmost precision are necessary. The alternative is to create bitterness, jealousy, and confusion among one's subordinates because of overlapping responsibilities.

Along with the delegation of responsibility there must be a delegation of authority, for without authority, subordinates will be seriously handicapped in the execution of their duties. This means that they will not only be given plans to implement, but they will also be given the power to initiate and carry such plans through to their completion. Hence, the necessary authority must be delegated so that the decisions to be made in connection with the execution of plans will be possible at every organizational level. This implies, too, the delegation of responsibility for planning to delegatees, and of authority *sufficient* for the execution of plans.

Assuming that the executive wishes to delegate, one may conclude that there will be a loosening of the strings of authority and of planning privileges. But there is no value in delegating responsibility without equivalent or commensurate authority. As Upson has so wryly commented:

> Delegation of administrative authority means actually delegating it — not merely saying that you do, and then trying to outsmart your subordinates on every technical subject that comes up. If you do, they will quit trying to be competent on the general

---

[7] Upson, *Letters on Public Administration*, pp. 33, 34.

theory that you are General Know-It-All and will make the decisions anyway.[8]

For example, if a board or administrator should delegate the responsibility for planning a Sunday-school visitation program to the assistant Sunday-school superintendent, authority must be given him to contact those who will share in the program, to request additional help from the church secretary, and to purchase the necessary materials. But to delegate a responsibility of this kind *without* the authority to do the above-mentioned things would severely limit him so that for all practical purposes he would be unable to discharge his assigned responsibility. If an executive is reluctant to delegate authority because he does not trust the judgment and ability of his subordinate, then let him train the subordinate or seek a more qualified person.

Along with the risk involved in delegating responsibility and authority, there is another matter which the executive must anticipate: he must be prepared to accept the blame if tasks are poorly performed, since ultimate responsibility cannot be delegated.[9]

In reference to the process of delegation in the Armed Services, we have the same principle reiterated:

> Every subordinate who exercises delegated authority commands. But that authority is delegated from somewhere. Finally the function of command must lead back to the principal executive officer; *the responsibility cannot be divorced from his personality.*[10]

An executive cannot, therefore, grant exclusive authority to a subordinate for the performance of a task and absolve himself of all responsibility. Inevitably, authority and responsibility which have been granted by the delegator will return to him. Because human behavior is unpredictable and because procrastination is a tendency on the part of human beings everywhere, the good executive will recognize that he is ultimately responsible for the performance of tasks which he delegates and will request oral or written reports on the projects which he assigns.

[8] *Ibid.,* p. 44.
[9] Newman, *Administrative Action,* p. 171.
[10] Gulick and Urwick, *Papers on the Science of Administration,* p. 77. (Italics supplied.)

In this way he can keep himself informed on the progress of duties which have been delegated to others.

Oftentimes the judgment of subordinates is found to be defective. If it is not this which plagues the administrator, it may very likely be the ambition of a subordinate who becomes domineering as soon as he receives authority, thereby creating widespread resentment within the staff. A clear statement, however, of the limits of a person's authority will help to prevent such tensions and misunderstandings from developing among staff personnel, especially when the limits are put into written form.

Training for Delegation

Most administrators are aware of the principle of delegation. They know that an organization can accomplish more, and that they themselves can become more efficient as they delegate responsibilities. The problem has not been a lack of knowledge about the value of delegation, but one of persuading others to *accept* the responsibilities which ought to be delegated. Not a few persons, when asked to share in the work of an organization, communicate either by word or facial expression the attitude that the administrator is trying to "pass the buck" or shirk some of the duties for which he was chosen. The average person cannot, or simply refuses, to reflect upon the line of demarcation between the duties an administrator should carry and those which he ought to delegate. Subconsciously most people recognize that the administrator cannot do everything; they nevertheless act as though he should.

Delegation becomes an even more difficult undertaking when in a growing organization the administrator must ask people to assume responsibilities which he has up to that time been accustomed to carry himself. To explain this to a church where a continual expansion of services and membership demands increasing delegation on the part of an administrator is no easy task. Only when one has allocated sufficient time for a job analysis by hours in the day and days in the week, and only when one has put the multiplied organizational relationships into pictorial form and discussed these with the appropriate boards,

can the "right atmosphere" be developed for successful delegation. Then, and only then, will an organization come to realize
the necessity of relieving the administrator of some of his duties.
(Again, see Figure 8, p. 67, for an example of a work distribution
form.)

Tead has recommended such job analyses on a periodic basis
for efficient organization:

> The written formulation of a comprehensive series of executive
> job analyses is of crucial value. Experience shows that in the
> formulation of these the executives involved should have an
> active part and that final adoption of each such job analysis
> should, at the top level, be a matter for review and acceptance
> by one's staff equals and co-workers, by the head administrators,
> and by the individual executive himself. Also, periodic re-exa-
> mination of these statements of duties should be made to be
> sure that, as ongoing activities inevitably alter the demands upon
> each executive, all newly required responsibilities are clearly
> allocated.[11]

Of course, one can decide to do things himself if he wishes.
This often seems to be the easy way out of an administrative
dilemma. One may even convince himself that things will only
be done properly if he does them; whereas to delegate only
creates problems and results in his ultimately doing the things
which he had hoped a subordinate could adequately handle.
This is a fallacy in thinking, however, and is not uncommon. As
Upson has remarked:

> The maxim, "To have a thing well done, do it yourself," has no
> place in the science of administration. By definition, administra-
> tion is getting things done through others.[12]

If one is to continue to enlarge his organization's area of
service, and if one is going to devote himself to the more important obligations, he must learn to delegate. Is this not the
principle that the apostles themselves used as the church in
Jerusalem increased in size? Note what Luke tells us:

> Now in these days when the disciples were increasing in number,
> the Hellenists murmured against the Hebrews because their
> widows were neglected in the daily distribution. And the twelve
> summoned the body of the disciples and said, "It is not right

[11] Ordway Tead, *The Art of Administration,* p. 107.
[12] L. D. Upson, *Letters on Public Administration,* 1954, p. 13.

that we should give up preaching the word of God to serve tables. Therefore, brethren, pick out from among you seven men of good repute, full of the Spirit and of wisdom, whom we may appoint to this duty. But we will devote ourselves to prayer and to the ministry of the word" (Acts 6:1-4).

To pray and to study the Word of God were not the only responsibilities of the apostles, but the principle which they recognized was that some things are more important than others. They were persuaded that their responsibility was to give themselves to those matters which were the most important to their ministry. Other duties and activities were to be delegated to capable individuals.

Now by what methods can people in our day be prepared or trained to accept delegated responsibilities? Here are several approaches which have been tested and proven fruitful.[13]

Example-Setting Approach

In this method, the executive arranges for potential leaders to observe him at work in a number of different situations. These leadership candidates may even assist him in minor projects. But their primary function is to observe him as he works and arrives at decisions. They will note how he weighs the pros and cons of an argument, how he will weigh one item against another and then come to a definite decision. In short, they will take note of the dynamics of decision-making, of planning, and of leadership in general.

For this reason many ministers-to-be are anxious to work in a large church under a successful pastor. Instead of learning administrative methodology and leadership behavior patterns by trial-and-error, they can learn these things vicariously through careful observation. Five years of experience, for example, under a successful administrator are worth perhaps ten years or more of experience in a situation where there is no example to be studied, and where one must learn the principles of human relations and executive leadership through hard and bitter experience.

In the training of lay personnel for responsibility in the

13 This material has been adapted from *The Executive Life*, pp. 142-144.

church, the example-setting approach is of great value, even as it is in the commercial world. And is this not the method our Lord used when He gathered the disciples around Himself for three years, instructing them until they were ready to lead the church which He established and for which He lived and died?

Group-Interaction Approach

In addition to the preparation of men for sharing in the process of delegation through the example-setting approach and its accompanying method of observation, the administrator may further prepare his lay people by encouraging their membership on committees and boards. As these groups meet, the administrator may direct simple but stimulating questions to these men. "What would you say, Jim, to the proposal that we have just made?" the minister might ask in a group situation. With this type of question the man in training will be forced to begin thinking in those ways expected of leaders. It may be at first that the administrator will direct a question to one of these men and, if no reply is immediately forthcoming, quickly suggest an answer. This will help prevent any embarrassment on the part of the one questioned. However, at a subsequent time the administrator may direct another question to the same individual with the expectation that he will be better prepared for contributing in a constructive way to the discussion, thereby learning from the experience.

Informal-Control Approach

A third method involves the assignment of a challenging project to a potential leader. He is not left alone with this project, however. A number of informal conferences are planned so that in the course of events the administrator actually suggests each step in the project. The outcome of this approach is increased confidence on the part of the delegatee who feels that he himself has carried the project almost single-handedly. It will also give him added experience in preparation for similar operations in the future. Success, of course, is essential for the potential leader during the early stages of his leadership efforts.

Discouragement or failure at the outset will often result in the loss of a potential leader or his reluctance to assume responsibility at future dates. The attitude that potential leaders, whether young or old, should "taste failure as well as success," is only true *after* a sufficient momentum of success has been experienced. Then, when failure is encountered, its effects can be offset by a backlog of successes and thus contribute to the maintenance of confidence and self-assurance.

Assignment-with-Freedom Approach

This is perhaps the most demanding, and yet the most rewarding of the approaches presented. It involves assigning a major responsibility to a potential leader and allowing him to fulfill it without any formal or informal controls. It is the method with the greatest risk inasmuch as success or failure is dependent upon the trainee's skills and resourcefulness. Assistance, of course, should not be withheld from one who has been assigned to a pressure-type situation; help should always be available to anyone who seeks it. But assistance is offered in the same degree to which it is available to others in similar leadership positions. The assigned situation may be a project which involves starting a new class, sponsoring a new youth group, organizing a social activity, or planning a special program. It is wise, however, to assign only those duties and projects which are special rather than routine in nature. This is due to the fact that permanent personnel often resent any transfer of their routine duties to other persons, but will gladly welcome newcomers who will assume new or special duties in the group. Whatever the nature of the project assigned, there should be a great deal of freedom and flexibility afforded the person to whom the responsibility is given.

Is there a time when the administrator or supervisor should perform some of the tasks which he has delegated to others, especially after he has trained others through various methods to accept the delegated responsibilities? Pfiffner has said:

> The good supervisor spends more of his time on supervisory activities *per se*. These include planning, scheduling, making out reports, seeing that materials are on hand, and liaison with

85

people outside of the immediate work group. The supervisor will get higher group production if he engages in expediting activities rather than performing production work himself. There are places for working supervisors, and it may occasionally be salutary for the supervisor to pitch in and by example motivate his group. Nevertheless, it is normally much better for him to supervise rather than do his journeyman stint.[14]

The point of all this is simply to say that the good administrator is one who trains others to receive delegated assignments. Obviously, there will be times when he will feel a responsibility to participate in carrying out some of the projects himself. He will feel a responsibility to motivate others with his example. But generally speaking he should devote himself to those activities which will keep the organization running smoothly and efficiently, which will keep morale at a high level and will permit him to devote himself to the more important activities.

Preventing Mistakes

When an administrator has delegated a responsibility, this does not imply that he should have no more concern for the proper discharge of that responsibility. On the contrary, he is always responsible in the ultimate sense for all that goes on under his jurisdiction. It is important, therefore, that he train his personnel so that they will perform their tasks effectively. But training is not the end of the delegation process. There are other aspects of delegation. There must also be techniques, for example, for assessing the progress of subordinates. The good administrator sets up a system of controls whereby he not only trains his personnel but also evaluates their work regularly:

> The good delegator is also a good organizer. The supervisor analyzes the work to be done and makes job breakdowns. He conducts job analyses and assigns to others the work which he does not have to do himself. He then lets these people know what is expected of them in quite definite terms. But he does not stop there, because he sets up controls consisting of a flow of information of a follow-up nature.[15]

[14] J. M. Pfiffner, *The Supervision of Personnel*, p. 222.
[15] *Ibid.*, pp. 268-269.

It is, then, one thing to know the ways available for delegating responsibilities and preparing men to accept such duties as may be assigned them, but it is an entirely different matter to *prevent mistakes* by those who have been given assignments.

Informal Communications

What check can be employed in guiding delegatees so that their mistakes will be kept to a mimimum and of a relatively harmless nature?

For one thing, a system of informal communication should be employed. If only formal channels are used, people develop a feeling that the church is a machine and that they are simply cogs in the machinery. However, if an informal approach is utilized, this general feeling can be averted. The administrator should make an effort to visit personally each of the divisions of his organization, and talk to his co-workers informally, discussing with them the problems which perplex them. This same feeling-out process should be conducted at committee and luncheon engagements. As a matter of fact, wherever groups of an informal or semi-formal nature meet, the administrator should be constantly prepared to receive or impart information which will contribute toward making the delegation process more effective.

Brief Reports

The administrator may decide also that brief written reports be submitted to him from selected committee meetings. In this way he can maintain contact with those groups which are formulating plans — plans which at some future date may interfere with certain projected plans of the organization. As we have previously indicated (p. 60) many decisions must be made and many long-range plans must be formulated at the lower levels of the hierarchy. Oftentimes these plans may be inadequately developed or may conflict with the plans of those at other levels of the organizational structure.

For example, a pastor may have delegated the planning of all church choir activities to his Director of Music. Included in the program each year is a week-end retreat in the early fall which leaves the church without the services of the choir from Friday evening through Sunday. But for some reason, the choir has decided to plan its retreat this year for a week-end other than the customary one. The pastor, not knowing of the change, schedules a Home-Coming Program for the same Sunday that the choir will be away. Conceivably, these decisions could take place six to eight months in advance if long-range planning characterized the work of both the choir and the church staff. If the pastor felt the need for the choir's presence at the projected Home-Coming, as might be expected, and if he desired to avoid misunderstandings and tensions at a later date, any written report dispatched to him immediately after the choir's planning session would alert him to the existing problem and would provide him with ample time for contacting the music director and making other arrangements more suitable to all parties.

It is, therefore, of the utmost importance that future plans be communicated (either orally or in writing) to those administering the church, if activities are to be coordinated and problems kept to a minimum.

Interlocking Ex-officio Memberships

Of course, situations such as the one just described might easily be avoided through a system of interlocking ex-officio memberships, whereby the members of the church staff attend important board meetings regularly and through their attendance gain information which can be reported at the weekly meeting of the entire staff. In the event that the church staff is too small for this kind of operation, then the church organizational structure should be such as to permit a representative from each of the major boards and committees to sit in on that group which is the highest policy-making body of the church.

Although one may not feel a particular system of interlocking memberships is best for his church, nevertheless the practice is a sound one. In the General Motors Corporation, this principle was employed by Harlow Curtis when he was president of that large business enterprise. Arrangements were made so that *selected* men from lower-echelon committees were members also of middle-echelon committees and those who were members of middle-echelon committees were members of upper-echelon committees. Through this method information moved up the hierarchy to the president through persons as well as written reports.[16]

Handbooks of Procedure

A final method is that of providing handbooks to guide program personnel. This is much better than word-of-mouth instructions and superior to putting down assignments or definitions of duties in the minutes of a committee, the latter frequently being inaccessible when needed. The clear, printed statement of duties and responsibilities in a widely distributed handbook will do much toward eliminating vagueness about one's job. It will also aid in preventing abuses of one's authority and the resultant overstepping of job boundaries. As Newman has said:

> One of the chief difficulties with respect to authority is a failure to recognize the limitations, either expressed or implied, that surround almost every delegation. Too often, an executive just "gives the necessary authority" to perform a vague group of activities without seriously considering the matter at all. In other cases, the executive has fairly definite ideas in mind, but fails to make these clear to his subordinate and others affected.[17]

Moreover, a good handbook will reduce the number of persons seeking "reinstruction" in their responsibilities, since the basic material will be in printed form for them to read and review. Also, written instructions become a means of internal control, in that responsibility can be determined if, and when, the expected results are not forthcoming. The value of this approach has been given by Pfiffner:

> In the first place, checks will be better accepted if it is known that management policy requires and expects them. Hence, the principal internal checks should be written, coupled with definition of who is to check and who is to be checked. Delegation should be accompanied by internal checks, which, if properly articulated and reported, will furnish the supervisor with

---

[16] *Executive Life*, pp. 145-146.
[17] Newman, *op. cit.*, p. 166.

the information he could otherwise acquire only by constantly peering over shoulders.[18]

Delegation to individuals, therefore, requires careful planning and precise assignments accompanied by methods which help in checking the performance of those within the organization.

Delegation of Responsibilities to Committees

It is not always to particular persons that responsibilities are delegated. On the contrary, sometimes committees will be appointed to carry out specific functions. Committees may be defined as groups of persons specifically designed to perform some administrative act. There are both temporary and permanent committees, and there are those with or without chairmen.

If the principle of unity of management is followed, then for the sake of efficiency every committee whether of a temporary nature or not should have an appointed or elected chairman. Even the committee with a chairman will encounter difficulties, but the committee *without* a chairman will experience far greater difficulties and manifest indecision and irresponsibility. As the President's Committee on Administrative Management in the Federal Government has observed:

> For purposes of management, boards and commissions have turned out to be failures. Their mechanism is inevitably slow, cumbersome, wasteful, and ineffective. . . . The conspicuously well-managed administrative units in the Government are almost without exception headed by single administrators.[19]

Though the quotation above indicates a disenchantment with committee work, it should be noted that it was a *committee* that brought in the report! In other words, a committee can be useful even while it is in the process of criticizing the efficiency of committees.

It is well for anyone concerned with administration to be thoroughly familiar with both the advantages and also disadvantages of committee work. Some of those commonly given are listed below.

[18] Pfiffner, *op. cit.*, p. 112.
[19] Quoted by Urwick in *Elements of Administration*, p. 71.

Disadvantages of Committees

1. In comparison to a single administrator, committees are usually much slower and require the time of a great many persons. This disadvantage may be minimized if the chairman will prepare an agenda before the meeting and distribute it to the members of the committee for their study. Another method for conserving time is to set a limit of 20 minutes for the discussion of an agenda item. If the item cannot be handled in the stipulated period, it may be referred to a subcommittee or tabled for future consideration.

2. Committees tend to divide responsibility so that no single individual accepts the blame for any failure of the committee to carry out its assignment. Each member accuses the other of "failing to cooperate," "refusing to be reasonable," or "setting obstacles in the way." One way to avoid this weakness is to require the secretary to keep comprehensive minutes, recording the positions of individual members in voting so that responsibility can be more easily fixed.

3. There is always danger of compromise for the sake of reaching some kind of decision. Under certain circumstances, committee members may feel that *any* decision is better than none, in view of the time and energy which have been invested. To make matters worse, there may also be great social pressure from persons outside the committee for the committee to "quit stalling," "settle its differences," and "come up with a decision." Compromise is oftentimes the result of these pressures and attitudes.

4. Although a committee is sometimes more considerate than a single person in evaluating the capabilities of someone in the church program, it is also true that it may *not* be as considerate. For example, Mrs. Smith is transferred or dismissed from her position not by the pastor, educational director, or Sunday school superintendent, but by "a committee." When Mrs. Smith seeks to discover why she was dismissed, and by whom, she may encounter obscurantism in the form of "it was the vote of the committee." This is a method frequently used to handle unpleasant tasks without an individual's being held responsible, but

for this very reason committee decisions can, and do, often result in unfairness and injustice.

5. Finally, a committee cannot lead effectively. It is well known to students of psychology that a crowd cannot follow two or three persons who have *equal authority*. Our Lord stated this principle when He said, "No one can serve two masters; for either he will hate the one and love the other, or he will be devoted to the one, and despise the other" (Matt. 6:24). If, on the other hand, a chairman is elected, a committee becomes somewhat more effective, depending upon the degree of authority and power granted him. To be without a committee chairman is but to invite difficulty. Barnard has remarked that "in conditions of complexity, or great danger, or rapidity of action, they [people] have rarely been willing or able to follow a committee . . . ."[20]

Advantages of a Committee

Because committee work is becoming increasingly important in our churches and because it is part of our democratic way of life, the administrator should weigh the advantages against the disadvantages and attempt to formulate a philosophy which describes the circumstances under which varying degrees of democratic leadership may be employed.

1. If an important decision affecting the entire church is to be rendered, then the widest range of experience and knowledge, represented in a well-chosen committee, should be obtained before the final decision is made. Proverbs tells us that "in an abundance of counselors there is safety" (Prov. 11:14b). Individual counselors frequently disagree; their information seems to conflict. It therefore becomes the responsibility of a committee to gather, sift, and interpret information and advice from many sources and analyze these with the aim of reaching a satisfactory decision. A committee with broad representation would be essential, for instance, in reaching a decision on the relocation of a church, since this type of action would demand various kinds of data and would affect the lives of the entire membership.

[20] Chester I. Barnard, "Dilemmas of Leadership in the Democratic Process," *Human Relations in Administration*, p. 235.

2. A committee is also useful for evaluating the operation of a program. One evaluator's judgment might reveal prejudice and personal bias. Or, because of an individual's limited knowledge of all the areas in a program (for example, one might be familiar with youth and adult work but would be unacquainted with children's work), it would be necessary to include others in the appraisal.

Moreover, if all aspects of a Christian education program were to be appraised, the magnitude of the operation might suggest additional personnel for this task as a way of economizing on time. Certainly a *thorough* evaluation of all facilities, equipment, supplies, curriculum, and teaching procedures would require 50 to 100 or more hours of work. Few persons would have this much time available for an uninterrupted, efficient evaluation program. A committee, therefore, or a team of appraisers would be unquestionably necessary for a task of this nature.

3. Committees are also valuable in the establishment of general policies. It may be the selection of a curriculum or the formulation of a leadership training program, but whatever the policy to be considered, if it affects a cross-section of the personnel in the educational program of the church, the combined judgment of the various department heads would be in order. Neglecting to include such persons in policy formulation is running the risk of opposition and possible rejection of any recommended changes in the future. It is commonly known that leaders are usually suspicious of programs in which they themselves have not participated at the policy-making level and are reluctant in such circumstances to put them into operation.

4. As previously mentioned in this chapter (p. 84), committees are valuable learning devices for potential but inexperienced leaders. While these leaders attend committee meetings, they can acquaint themselves with the unique problems of the church, with the philosophy of the church, and with the personality dynamics of the present leaders, all of which will prepare them for future leadership in the church.

5. Committees may also function in the coordination of the church program in so far as they become "clearinghouses" for ideas and proposed actions. Of course, truly effective coordi-

nation will be accomplished by a committee to the extent that it authorizes the chairman or some other member to carry out such action as is needed.

Summary

It is not possible for one person to conduct all of the business of a church. He must have assistance. The crucial question facing the minister (or other administrative officer) centers around the apportionment of responsibilities. What criteria will enable the administrator to assign certain duties and retain others so that *maximum* benefit will come to the church?

Some of the principles which will aid the minister-executive in answering the above question have been spelled out in detail in this chapter. Among the principles which were presented, the following would appear to deserve special consideration.

1. The larger an organization becomes, the more an administrator must concern himself with policies and procedures and the less he will concern himself with specific details.

2. The effective administrator delegates the less important duties and responsibilities and retains the more important ones.

3. The delegation of responsibility demands that commensurate authority also be delegated.

4. The sharing of responsibility through delegation with a person or committee does not release the delegator from ultimate responsibility.

5. The good administrator employs a training program for the education of potential leaders, with a view to the delegation of responsibilities to such persons when the organization is in need of their services.

6. The establishment of standard practices for the operation of an organization and the setting down of delegated duties in writing (which are usually incorporated in a handbook) should permit the administrator to spend more time in creative activity.

A training program, as our fifth principle states, is a vital aspect of the administrator's program. How to identify and recruit prospective leaders — one of the most difficult tasks in the church — is the topic of our next chapter.

References to Administrative Techniques in Appendix

1. Techniques 4 and 5 show how duties are delegated through policy-making statements.
2. The importance of delegation for the operation of the Sunday church school and vacation church school may be noted in Techniques 10 and 12.

V

Leadership

Recruitment and Enlistment

There is probably no greater administrative responsibility than that of providing competent leadership for a church's educational program. To a great extent, the success of a church program depends upon the abilities of the leaders — the superintendents, the teachers, the sponsors and other workers. If they are untrained in communication and in the use of educational methods and materials, even the finest equipment and curriculum will prove to be ineffective. The best-planned program will fail miserably without the necessary leadership to administer it. If a church is enlarging its program, it becomes all the more important that capable leadership be placed in the positions of greatest responsibility, since the pastor will of necessity be compelled to delegate to other individuals the administration of certain areas over which he may have previously had close supervision. Since it is no easy task to remove or transfer a person from an office to which he may have been appointed, the administrator must make every effort to avoid the placement of personnel in key positions until he has satisfied himself that the best available persons have been chosen. This is one point at which the administrator can beneficially apply the proverb, "An ounce of prevention is worth a pound of cure." Precautions taken before the appointment of personnel will greatly reduce the number of possible dismissals or administrative changes at a later date. The responsibility for the identification, recommendation, preparation, and evaluation of candidates for leadership positions should, of course, be that of the pastor or educational director, assisted by the Board or Committee of Christian Education.

Certainly the matter of leadership selection and development should not be neglected nor left to chance. Though there are many things we do not understand about the nature and development of leadership, we must nevertheless employ the knowledge which is available and constantly seek to improve the programs which have been started. This is by no means a simple undertaking, especially in a voluntary organization. Most pastors will agree that the recruitment and training of volunteer leaders is perhaps the most difficult assignment in the work of the church.

Background for Recruitment

A careful analysis of the scheduled activities in a church week will indicate that between one-half and three-quarters of these are centered in educational efforts. Many of the personnel serve in a voluntary capacity and function as Sunday school teachers, youth group sponsors, leaders of boys' and girls' groups, instructors in released-time religious education classes and other similar activities. If such a large part of the church's program is educational in nature, it becomes essential for the pastor and other church leaders to give the educational task of the church the time and consideration it deserves. But if a minimum of time is given to the discussion of educational matters by the official church boards, if only a limited amount of space is devoted to education in the church bulletin, if the pastor rarely gives attention to the educational program in his announcements on Sundays, church members will develop (at least subconsciously) the impression that education is an insignificant activity within the total church program. The logical outcome of such an approach will be the general reluctance of members to serve in the ministry of teaching since it appears to be of minor importance with regard to the time and space which the pastor and others devote to it.

Only when an "educational climate" is produced within the church will people feel the obligation to serve in the teaching ministry. But this kind of atmosphere can be created by a pastor and his staff only after they are personally convinced of the vital function of the teaching ministry in reaching those outside the church and instructing those already within its fold. When this type of background for education has been established, it then becomes an easy matter to approach lay people about serving in various positions of responsibility. Church members will recognize that the church is truly the Body of Christ (I Cor. 12) and that each individual has a part in fulfilling the plan of God through service in his own church as well as in the world.

Who Should Recruit?

In the smaller church where no educational director serves, it will undoubtedly be the pastor who will bear the major responsibility for discovering and training leaders. If it is a moderately large church, the pastor may find that the Sunday school superintendent is capable of sharing or completely assuming this task. Or, in the event that the church organization includes a Board of Christian Education, this responsibility may be delegated to one of its members. If the latter is done, the responsibility for *nominating* teachers and other Christian education workers should be given to a particular board member, while the right to *approve* such nominations should be reserved for the entire Board.

In large churches the Board of Christian Education will very likely include the educational director as a voting or ex-officio member, and the responsibility for nominating prospective workers will fall to him. In the event that a church is without a director, the chairman of the Board or the Sunday school superintendent could accept this duty. The entire board, however, should vote the approval of any nominations made. This is in general agreement with administrative practice which dictates that boards set policies and approve personnel, whereas superintendents or other official staff members who execute policies simply nominate the personnel who are to serve in the organization. Reeder has stated: "Actually, the superintendent should nominate, and the board should *appoint*."[1] The principle of nomination by an administrator and approval by a board prevails in our public schools. It is in line with general organizational theory and should be followed in our churches. As Sorenson has said in his *Art of Board Membership*: "The board *confirms, modifies,* or *rejects* executive or committee proposals."[2] In most of our churches, though a board or committee might assume responsibility for the program of leadership recruitment and training, the pastor will still be expected to cooperate closely in this crucial task. There are many times when only he, as the chief executive officer of the church, can offer the help and encouragement a prospective leader desires before giving his consent to serve in a church office.

Identifying Leaders for the Church

The first step in the recruitment of leaders is that of determining the general characteristics of a Christian leader. Although the following list is not exhaustive, it may provide guidance.

He Should Be Spiritual

This quality may not be considered essential for leadership in the business world, but it is absolutely imperative for work in the cause of Christ. It should be noted, however, that Barnard feels that morality — which is not identical to, but is included in spirituality — is an important part even in business enterprises. He says: "A low morality will not sustain leadership long; its influence quickly vanishes, it cannot produce its own succession."[3] How much more important it is that the man in a position of church leadership display not only a high morality but also claim to have had an encounter with Jesus Christ, an encounter in which he has made Him his Lord and Savior. No man can serve satisfactorily as a channel of God's message if he does

[1] Ward Reeder, *The Fundamentals of Public School Administration*, p. 111.
[2] Roy Sorenson, *Art of Board Membership*, p. 31.
[3] Barnard, *Functions of the Executive*, p. 283.

not have the inner resources and deep personal experience with Christ for rightly interpreting that message to others. Without these resources and this experience, he would be as wells without water and as clouds without rain. Spirituality, therefore, is the primary prerequisite to leadership within the church.

He Should Be Educable

That is, he should possess the necessary native capacities for becoming a leader. Even though his educational background may be limited, if he can learn quickly, make sound judgments within the sphere to which he is accustomed, and display an interest in assuming additional responsibility, he may well be considered a potential church leader. Though these qualities are admittedly only partial measures of one's educability, they do provide a clue for determining the degree to which this trait is present. The importance of these qualities cannot be overemphasized since they are needed in all areas of life. Three other aspects of educability should also be present: he should be able to speak, read, and write well. Chapman has declared:

> Management is deeply involved in the art of communication and often success and profit depend upon it. Eventually, all decisions must be communicated, either orally or in writing. The ability to express oneself and the ability to understand what is expressed are absolute prerequisites for successful executive performance. At the very top, the man who cannot express himself will not be successful; for it is he who must communicate the essential meaning of business decisions and policies to all levels. . . . Without the ability to read intelligently and write coherently, the young man is not a prospect for executive responsibility. A career in industrial leadership offers no prospect of reward to him.[4]

He Should Be Cooperative

It is rather common knowledge today that there are as many persons dismissed from their jobs in the secular world due to lack of social understanding and inability to get along with

[4] Gilbert W. Chapman in *Toward the Liberally Educated Executive*, edited by Robert Goldwin and Charles A. Nelson, New American Library, 1960 (Mentor Book), pp. 11-12.

others as to a lack of knowledge or technical competence. Therefore, one cannot overlook the compatibility index of persons within an organization. The organization with technically capable but uncooperative and intolerant persons will not be nearly as productive as one with persons slightly less capable but cooperative, tolerant, and understanding. This is what Bernard means when he says:

> The general method of maintaining an informal executive organization is so to operate and to select and promote executives that a general condition of compatibility of personnel is maintained. Perhaps often and certainly occasionally men cannot be promoted or selected, or even must be relieved, because they cannot function, because they "do not fit," where there is no question of formal competence. This question of "fitness" . . . represents in its best sense the political aspects of personal relationship in formal organization. I suspect it to be most highly developed in political, labor, church, and university organizations, for the very reason that the intangible types of personal services are relatively more important in them than in most other, especially industrial, organizations. But it is certainly of major importance in all organizations.[5]

It would be naive to think that those incapable of social adaptation remain outside our church doors. If some ninety million Americans belong to church organizations it is quite likely that the churches contain a fairly good cross-section of American life, including every type of the socially adaptable and unadaptable. It becomes incumbent upon nominating committees (with, no doubt, a socially unadaptable member or two in the group) to select those persons who would most likely develop the organization's program at a maximum level. This is not to be construed as the rejection of any person. It does imply, however, that those charged with the selection of leaders must prayerfully and humbly seek to determine the place where each member can serve best in the Body of Christ.

If there are some who are better qualified to work with people than are others, then they should be given those positions most in consonance with their abilities. Chapman has stated that the levels of management must be manned "by people

[5] Barnard, *op. cit.*, p. 224.

who understand others. This is the key to leadership."[6] For those who work in God's vineyard, we can say that this ability is surely *one* of the most important leadership keys. Other qualities, of course, are also crucial to good leadership in the service of Christ.

He Should Possess a Spirit of Dedication

This quality may be defined as the action of committing oneself to a program and to those who are in that program. When one dedicates himself to God, he sets himself apart for God's work. He commits himself to the plan which God has designed. If one is connected with a particular group, he can exert every effort to influence the development of the group's program. But once it has been voted or enacted, he should then dedicate himself to its implementation.

Both responsibility and loyalty will usually be present in a dedicated person: responsibility, in that when he accepts an assignment he will, despite all obstacles, complete it according to plan; loyalty, in that he accepts the program as his, and is true to the program even to the execution of the minutest detail. Why are these qualities necessary? Because without responsibility and without loyalty the "lines of communication cannot function at all unless the personal contributions of executives will be present at the required positions, at the times necessary, without default for ordinary personal reasons."[7] Everyone is in need of limited assistance, it is true. But the person who must receive constant guidance and who appears not only indifferent to his responsibilities but deliberately unfaithful to the program might better serve in positions of little or no responsibility until such time as he is prepared to assume his due share of the work load in a spirit of trust and dedication.

He Should Display Enthusiasm

Enthusiasm is contagious. It influences others so that they become interested in things which may have held little concern for them before. But just what is enthusiasm? It is a quality

[6] Chapman, *op. cit.*, p. 12.
[7] Barnard, *op. cit.*, p. 220.

102

of mind characterizing a person who finds enjoyment in pursuing a goal. Most persons enjoy doing those things which they can do successfully and which will give them a sense of achievement. In addition, enthusiasm manifests itself in certain overt ways. These include the gestures of arms and hands, the inflections of the voice, and the expressions on the face. One may enjoy doing certain things (which is the first step in developing enthusiasm) but he must also *demonstrate* his feeling of enjoyment in ways perceptible to others.

Even though one may be well educated, and may have had previous work experience, if he lacks this quality it will be exceedingly difficult for him to function effectively in an important leadership position. This is particularly true for those who desire to work with young people. With their spirit of independence, young people are reluctant to attend church activities unless there is good, enthusiastic leadership. Adults, on the other hand, will tolerate a person who lacks enthusiasm, and children will endure such a person simply because they are too young to change their own circumstances. The ideal, of course, is to secure enthusiastic teachers and leaders for important positions at *all* age levels as much as this is humanly possible.

Job Descriptions

One of the most important principles in staffing an organization is that of fitting individuals to jobs rather than jobs to the individuals. The use of this principle contributes to organizational stability in that the structure will remain essentially the same from year to year even though the turnover in leadership may be relatively high. A low turnover, of course, is more desirable in that it adds even greater stability to an organization. If, however, the structure of an organization is constantly changing and a high turnover in personnel accompanies this, a sense of apprehension and insecurity may result. Loyal and experienced personnel begin to wonder what is going to happen *next*, and a lack of confidence in the leadership soon develops. Moreover, it is difficult to plan a leadership training program if new jobs are constantly being created and the duties connected with well-established offices are constantly being modified.

103

The point has been aptly made that it is not possible to plan for the rearing of future executives without knowing: (1) what duties they will be called upon to carry out, and (2) how many will be needed and when.[8]

It becomes imperative, therefore, to list the jobs which are presently part of the organizational structure and, moreover, to determine the additional jobs necessary for improved operations in the future. It is a matter of planning the "ideal" organizational structure, as Newman has indicated.[9] Of course, one must learn to break away long enough from his present habits of thinking and operation to reflect objectively about the problems of the organization and how it may be improved. If the administrator can begin by picturing in his mind an ideal organizational structure and set this as a goal, he will make progress in building what is probably a far more effective organization than he presently administers. · But it is a process of knowing how to visualize these matters and how to achieve them. Examples of the types of positions in a moderately large church are given in the figures in Chapter 2 in order to aid the reader in visualizing possible organizational changes. It is assumed that each church will make such modifications as are necessary for its own particular set of circumstances.

Along with a statement of positions in an organization and the accompanying duties, there should be an indication of the general qualities desired for each position. What kind of person is best suited for this job? Have the characteristics and traits that ought to be present in his personality been listed? What are the skills required for this position? How much training is necessary? These and similar questions should be answered as the qualities desired are put into written form. Since it is often difficult to secure the "ideal" person for positions in an organization, the person who meets the qualifications most satisfactorily should be selected. An alternative which is sometimes taken in the event that no available person even remotely satisfies the standards is to postpone the selection until someone has been trained or otherwise secured. Meanwhile an interim arrangement is employed.

[8] Pfiffner, *Supervision of Personnel*, p. 427.
[9] Newman, *Administrative Action*, p. 321.

Sources of Leadership

Where is one to obtain qualified leaders to fill positions in the educational program? To what sources may the pastor or administrator go for teachers, sponsors, and other educational workers? Some of the sources which have been found helpful in churches are as follows:

New Members

Perhaps the most fruitful source of leadership is the pastor's instruction class for new church members. In an interview with one of the staff members of the Moody Church in Chicago, the author learned that this method was most valuable in the recruitment of new leadership. In this class the pastor deals with the attitude a member should have toward his church (e.g., he should pray for the work of the church, support the church financially, etc.) and with the place each member has in the Body of Christ. He explains the purpose and the program of the church and the necessity for each member's participation in the program if it is to be effective. He then distributes questionnaires which list the types of jobs and positions in the program, with space provided for indicating the positions in which one prefers to serve. There are also questions which ask the new member to describe the amount of experience he has had in each of the job preferences. These forms are placed on file for future reference.

In the author's opinion, this is probably one of the most effective methods available for discovering, motivating, and enlisting leadership. What better time is there to impress upon church members their privilege and their responsibility to share in the work of Christ than at the time they become members of the church? Moreover, who could better present the purpose and program of the church than the pastor? For these reasons the church membership class is the most important source of leadership for an educational program. Figure 9 is an example of a typical church service recruitment form.

CHURCH SERVICE RECRUITMENT

Name   Tel.   Occupation   Bus. Tel.
(Last name, first name, middle initial)

Residence   Business Address
(Street, apt., or RFD) (City or town) (State) (Street or RFD) (City or Town) (State)

Age Group: Youth ☐; Young Adult ☐; Middle Adult ☐; Older Adult ☐.
       12-24   25-35   36-55   56 plus

Professional Training

I Have Served	Boards, Committees, and Officers	I Have Interest	I Have Served	Church Committees and Other Activities	I Have Interest
☐	Board of Deacons	☐	☐	Personnel Committee	☐
☐	Board of Deaconesses	☐	☐	Pulpit Supply Committee	☐
☐	Board of Trustees	☐	☐	Evangelism Committee	☐
☐	Finance Committee	☐	☐	Ushering Committee	☐
☐	Every Member Canvas Committee	☐	☐	Communications Committee	☐
☐	Board of Christian Education	☐	☐	Christian Social Progress Committee	☐
☐	Chairman of Children's Work	☐	☐	Auditing Committee	☐
☐	Chairman of Youth Work	☐	☐	Flower Committee	☐
☐	Chairman of Adult Work	☐	☐	Music Committee	☐
☐	Chairman of Missionary and Stewardship Education	☐	☐	Every Member Canvass Caller	☐
☐	Chairman of Leadership Education	☐	☐	Choir	☐
☐	Board or Committee of Missionary Promotion	☐	☐	Organist	☐
☐	Church Clerk	☐	☐	Choir Director	☐
☐	Church Treasurer	☐	☐	Music (Instrumental)	☐
☐	Financial Secretary	☐	☐	Visitation Evangelism	☐
☐	Church Historian	☐	☐	Recreation Leader	☐
☐	Church Librarian	☐	☐	Dramatic Coach	☐
☐	Sunday Church School Supt.	☐	☐	Teach Crafts	☐
☐	Instructor of Leadership Course	☐	☐	Lead Singing	☐
☐	Teacher in the Sunday Church School	☐	☐	Storytelling	☐
☐	Department Superintendent	☐	☐	General Office Work	☐
☐	Teacher in the Vacation Church School	☐	☐	Typing	☐
☐	Department Superintendent in the Vacation Church School	☐	☐	Teacher in the Sunday Church School	☐
☐	Teacher in the Weekday Church School	☐	☐	Department Superintendent	☐
☐	Leader in Baptist Sunday Evening Fellowship	☐	☐	Department Secretary	☐
☐	Department Secretary	☐	☐	Teacher in the Vacation Church School	☐
☐	Department Pianist	☐	☐	Teacher in the Weekday Church School	☐
☐	Leader of Weekday Club Activity	☐	☐	BYF Counselor	☐
	I am especially interested in the:		☐	Fellowship Guild Counselor	☐
☐	Nursery Department	☐	☐	Student-Service Personnel Counselor	☐
☐	Kindergarten Department	☐	☐	Pianist	☐
☐	Primary Department	☐	☐	Boys' Club Leader	☐
☐	Junior Department	☐	☐	Scoutmaster	☐
			☐	Member of Scouting Committee	☐
			☐	BYC Officer	☐
			☐	Advisor to BYF Emphasis Committees	☐
				Committee Member:	
			☐	Christian Faith	☐
			☐	Christian Witness	☐
			☐	Christian World Outreach	☐
			☐	Christian Citizenship	☐
			☐	Christian Fellowship	☐

NOTE: Possibly no church would have all of the activities listed on this card. Each church will provide the activities needed.

I am especially interested in the:

Figure 9.

I Have Served	Church Committees and Other Activities	I Have Interest	I Have Served	Other Services	I Have Interest
☐	Junior High Department	☐	☐	Teacher in the Sunday Church School	☐
☐	Senior High Department	☐	☐	Department Superintendent	☐
☐	Older Youth Department	☐	☐	Adult Class Officer	☐

I Have Served	Other Services	I Have Interest			
			☐	Discussion Leader in the Sunday Evening Fellowship	☐
☐	Visiting Sick and Shut-ins	☐	☐	Home Department Visitor	☐
☐	Visiting Prospective Members	☐	☐	Women's Society Officer	☐
☐	Entertaining Foreign Students	☐		Woman's Society Chairman:	
☐	Mimeographing	☐	☐	Love Gift	☐
☐	Addressing Envelopes	☐	☐	White Cross	☐
☐	Acting in Dramatic Productions	☐	☐	Christian Social Relations	☐
☐	Care for Costume Wardrobe	☐	☐	Program	☐
☐	Telephoning	☐	☐	House Party	☐
☐	Helping in the Kitchen	☐	☐	Literature	☐
☐	Providing or Arranging Flowers	☐	☐	Missionary and Stewardship Education for Women	☐
☐	Poster-making	☐			
☐	Painting	☐	☐	Speakers and Interpreters	☐
☐	Manual Work	☐	☐	Special Interest Missionaries	☐
☐	Electrial Work	☐	☐	Spiritual Life	☐
☐	Sewing	☐	☐	Family Life	☐
☐	Prayer for Persons in Need	☐	☐	Leadership Training for Women	☐
☐	Assisting the Sexton	☐	☐	Circle or Group Chairman	☐
☐	Securing Subscriptions for Religious Periodicals	☐	☐	Men's Fellowship Officer	☐
☐	Furnishing Transportation	☐	☐	Men's Fellowship Chairman	☐
☐	Welfare Work	☐	☐	Leader in Senior Adult Activities	☐
☐	Mission projects: Christian Center; Mission Sunday Church School, etc.	☐	☐	Lay Preaching	☐
			☐	Young Adult Group Leader	☐

In keeping with the principle of the "priesthood of believers," I believe that every member of the church should share in its life and work. It is my intent to serve the church as I may be able, in due consideration of the church's needs, and my own abilities and opportunities . . . I understand that the church will call on me to serve if and when needed for the activities I have checked.

Signature _____

Figure 9. From Church Service Recruitment Card, American Baptist Convention.

Church Officers

Usually the present or former officers of a church possess leadership traits which qualify them for service in educational leadership positions. In churches where board membership positions are rotated every two or three years so that a member has a "free" year, it may be possible to persuade a former board member to accept a teaching appointment or some other responsibility in the program even if it should be as a substitute teacher for a limited period of time.

Leadership Training Course Enrollees

A great many churches plan or participate in leadership training schools from time to time. Often these are conducted on an annual or semi-annual basis. Assuming that an interest in leadership is a primary factor to be considered in the selection of potential leaders, the individuals who enroll in these courses for the development of their abilities should be good prospects for sharing in the church's educational program. Most of the training courses offered in churches are open not only to those who are actively engaged in Christian work, but also to those interested in learning more about the Scriptures and the mission of the church. Because a knowledge of God's revelation to man as found in the Bible is essential for effective Christian service, one who has enrolled in leadership courses is more likely to possess an adequate foundation for church work than someone who has not enrolled in such courses. Furthermore, since attendance at such programs is purely voluntary, it may be assumed that enrollees are sufficiently motivated so that they would give serious consideration to a request for help in the church.

Sunday School Class Officers

One of the most productive areas of leadership talent is the Sunday school class. Here it is that a person who may have appeared an unlikely candidate for a leadership role can develop innate skills and capitalize on any aptitude he may have for leading others. In some churches, pastors and educational directors take particular note of class officers and their leadership ability in both the youth and adult departments. If there is a good chance that "Henry Brown" may become a capable leader, he is given opportunities and training which will permit him to develop his skills. As soon as his leadership abilities are sufficiently well developed, he may be asked to serve in an important office or to accept appointment to a responsible position.

A teacher may be somewhat resistant to the loss of a capable president or vice-president of his class to a teaching position in the Sunday school or some other responsible church job. In the final analysis, however, the teacher should recognize the vital role a leader (i.e., a teacher, sponsor, etc.) can play in building up the church of Christ and in reaching others with the message of hope and salvation.

Students in Christian Schools

Not every church is fortunate enough to be situated within five or ten miles of a Christian school. If, however, a Christian college or seminary should be within commuting distance, the pastor should make every effort to arrange for students, and perhaps available faculty members, to share in the church's educational program. This might require official sanction of the governing body of the church, but there is every reason to believe that the additional leadership would contribute greatly toward an aggressive program. Churches with sizable memberships, particularly those located in the center of large cities, find it imperative to obtain the very finest leadership, and therefore draw upon educational institutions in their areas. Several churches known to the author use school personnel in addition to their large full-time staffs because they realize that good leadership will contribute to a more effective program.

Church Visitors

There are millions of people who move from one home to another each year — estimates run as high as thirty million a year at the present time. Among this mobile population are persons with leadership ability, many of whom have served in church leadership positions. If these same leaders desire to continue using their leadership skills, they will not transfer their church membership upon arriving in a community. Rather, their psychological nature leads them to visit several churches in an effort to find the one in which they can serve most effectively. Such persons may visit a church for a period of five or six weeks. If no one visits their homes (or if someone does visit but fails to indicate an interest in their leadership potential), they tend to make visits to other churches until they discover one in which they can become actively engaged. For this reason it is best to ask visitors to register their presence at Sunday services. Then a church or staff member should make a friendly call and seek information relative to the person's background and church experience. This procedure could well produce new and vital leadership for a church. Therefore, let those charged with the responsibility of identifying and developing leadership not overlook the strangers who enter the doors of the church, for oftentimes such persons possess the spiritual gifts and skills for which a church has long been searching.

Enlistment of Leadership Personnel

How to Prepare

After listing the major characteristics desired in a candidate for a job, every effort should be made to locate him. To match the individual and the job is the goal. In the selection of public school teachers, Reeder suggests that "a teacher should be employed who will fit the position rather than to attempt to make the position fit the teacher."[10] This is no less true for the selection of church school teachers and other Christian education leaders.

If a prospect has refused to fill out a questionnaire indicating a desire to teach or sponsor a group, this should not be interpreted as a lack of interest. More often than not, those who submit forms and persistently seek positions of responsibility may not be as qualified as others who prefer that "the position seek the person rather than the person the position." If there is

[10] Reeder, *op. cit.*, p. 132.

110

evidence from several sources that an individual possesses certain capabilities, it may be assumed that he will at least be interested in discussing a position which would involve the use of his skills. (This is predicated on the fact that a person seldom develops skills in an area which holds no interest for him.)

The person chosen to conduct the interview should avoid speaking to the candidate in the presence of others. The period immediately after a church service is a poor time for an interview, for whenever there is the distraction of friends or of an impending engagement, the danger of failing to communicate the nature and importance of the task will be great. The ministry of serving Christ is a sacred task and deserves everyone's undivided attention. Since there is no method that can compare with the personal interview as a means of enlisting people in the work of the church, the most favorable circumstances should be sought. The personal, private approach was used time and again by our Lord, and the approach that we as His servants should use ought to be similar to His. The secular world has long recognized the validity of this approach as it has sent out its salesmen to make personal, face-to-face contacts with the public. All other things being equal, the more personal the contact made, the greater the possibility that an affirmative answer will be gained. Telephone calls and letters, though not to be overlooked, cannot compare with the effectiveness of a home visit made by the pastor or some other duly appointed person. Whoever does the interviewing should be certain to have a description of the job and a list of the persons who are connected with the position (e.g., the names of those in a class or group needing a teacher or sponsor). If these are typed on a 3 x 5″ card or on standard church stationery and given to the candidate, it will not only appear businesslike but will also serve as a reminder to him to consider seriously the opportunity for service that is before him.

On the other hand, a quick and thoughtless approach on the part of the interviewer will usually bring a hasty rejection. A candidate may for many reasons be fearful or suspicious of the unknown, and therefore refuse to consider the position which is open. "What is involved?" he asks. "How much time is this

111

going to take?" It is axiomatic that the more leadership ability a man possesses the more demands there will be for his time. If he is asked to commit himself to a task which is ill defined with respect to time and effort, he suspects that it may require *more* time than he has available. If the job description is complete, however, with some indication of the time factor and the obligations involved, he may consent to give it serious consideration and perhaps include it in his busy schedule.

The Interview

In approaching a potential teacher or leader, the interviewer may feel that he must follow the techniques of a "high-pressure salesman." This is not true in the least. If he has prepared himself with a working knowledge of the position to be filled, if he has prayed, and if he is inwardly convinced that the candidate is the person best qualified for the job, he should experience little difficulty in gaining acceptance. As he approaches the person, he must recognize and believe the truth that every Christian is part of the Body of Christ and has a function to fulfill in the church. Therefore, as he enters and speaks he should conduct himself as a servant of Christ seeking to place the candidate in the program of the church, so that his God-given gifts and skills will be appropriately employed.

After a few preliminary remarks, the pastor (or whoever is conducting the interview) should indicate the background of the call, describe the general discussion among the members of the board in reference to the particular position which needs to be filled, and make a statement to the effect that the board is persuaded that he, the candidate, should be approached. The interviewer should then proceed to outline the nature of the work, the time involved, the persons in the class or group, and the program materials which are available. Few persons desire to take the responsibility of directing a group without a specific curriculum — the time and creative ability necessary for drawing up a novel curriculum are not to be found in the average church member. It is imperative, therefore, to present the curriculum or program which is already obtainable for the group.

The candidate may at first appear to be reluctant, but if the curriculum materials are available so that he feels confident in respect to program planning, and if he is given an opportunity to handle the materials — this is important — and examine them so that the strangeness of the program is partially removed, he may then give tentative consent. No doubt some explanation of the use of the materials will be in order. If the interviewer is not sufficiently informed on the matter, as may be the case with a busy pastor, he should arrange to take someone from the board who has the knowledge for answering any questions that may arise. This is one basic reason that a telephone call or letter is so deficient. Without the materials in hand, questions regarding the curriculum to be used cannot be answered satisfactorily, and unfamiliarity with the curriculum can easily lead the candidate to refuse the opportunity being offered. Even students training for public school teaching are often fearful of possible failure in "working with the materials." The situations are different in many respects, of course, but certainly there is the element of strangeness, as well as concern, connected with the use of curriculum materials for the first time in Sunday church schools as in public school situations.

Some of the objections frequently given by candidates are these:

Inability. In such a case the pastor should assure the candidate that the committee feels he has the necessary ability at this point *to begin,* and with additional training in the leadership training courses he should become even more capable in his position.

Unfamiliar with Job. Along with an explanation of the use of the program material, there should be assurances that the departmental superintendent (if the matter discussed is a Sunday church school class), the educational director, or the chairman of the Board of Christian Education will work with the candidate for several weeks until such time as he feels able to handle the work independently.

Too Busy. This is seldom true with candidates, but if it should be the case, the question might be asked whether there should not be some adjustment in schedule. Behind this lies the question of priority for the work of God. The interviewer, and all Christians for that matter, should be absolutely convinced that the work of the church is the most important in the world because it (1) prepares us to live in right relationship with men here on earth and, more importantly, (2) prepares us to live with God for all eternity. Let us, then, stress a *top* priority for the work of Christ!

Lack of Transportation. In some sections of the country this is a critical problem. In other sections, public transportation is available, relatively efficient, and not an insurmountable obstacle. If, however, this problem seems almost insoluble, it would perhaps be best to recommend a position requiring the candidate's presence and leadership at the church one day a week. Under most circumstances this would have been previously considered by the committee and tentative arrangements made for transportation on the day involved.

Family Responsibilities. For many mothers and fathers, work connected with the support of the family and the care of children at home appear to preclude any active participation in the Christian education program other than attendance. Even so, *lesser responsibilities* can be suggested. Substitute teaching, addressing absentee cards, or serving as a social sponsor (allowing a youth group to visit one's home for an evening every third or fourth month) are examples. Frequently people who accept lesser responsibilities at first become the future leaders in the church as they become more and more acquainted with the objectives, the activities, and the people in the church program.

The pastor or educational director who conducts the interview should be prepared to present several possible jobs so that if the first is considered to be too much responsibility, a job of less responsibility may be suggested. The interviewer, therefore, should take with him a series of jobs with a descending requirement of time, energy, and skill. But *the attitude that should characterize the entire interview should be that of discovering what function in the Body of Christ this person should serve.* And if the contacts are made on a person-to-person basis, the solution to many of the leadership problems should soon be forthcoming.

114

Inducting the New Leader

Initial Guidance

In some churches it is customary to give the newly appointed leader an opportunity to visit the group with which he will work, so that he can develop a "feeling" for the philosophy of the program. This may be difficult to arrange, but it is a means of setting a high standard of performance if the chosen candidate can observe the program as it *should* be conducted. A departmental superintendent may teach the class, if that is the assignment, while the appointee observes. If the assignment is leading a young people's group, the retiring sponsor or Minister of Christian Education might direct the program, giving instruction to the new sponsor from time to time.

Perhaps the worst thing that could be done would be to allow the new leader to take up his responsibilities without any guidance whatsoever. If nothing more can be done in the way of assistance, the minimum help offered should consist of a Christian education handbook giving: (1) the objectives of the program, (2) how materials are ordered, (3) where audio-visual aids may be obtained, (4) the expected time of arrival for personnel at scheduled activities, (5) what to do in emergencies, (6) whom to call in case of illness, (7) how to keep the records, (8) the rules on attendance at business and other official meetings, and (9) who should be consulted for the solution of problems which arise from time to time. With this kind of oral and written assistance the newly selected leader should feel far more confident and assured than he would without such help.

Continuing Guidance

Even after the new leader has been serving for several weeks, the educational director or pastor should make periodic informal visits. The new leader may not expect any assistance but the mere fact that someone is interested in his progress as a servant of Christ will contribute to his morale. If this cannot be done, a Sunday church school teacher or one of the members of the Board of Christian Education should be assigned to the new worker so that helpful supervision is provided. The weekly or monthly Workers' Conference for Sunday school personnel is a means of assisting new teachers. But most important of all, whether the new leader be a teacher, a sponsor, or some other worker, he should feel that if assistance is needed there is an "open-door policy" on the part of the church staff.

References to Administrative Techniques in Appendix

1. Read the material in Technique 13 and observe how this program can prepare adults for possible leadership responsibility in the future.

2. Technique 14 is designed primarily for young people. Note the Biblical courses offered and the leadership skills which are represented in the curriculum.

3. A worker's covenant is given in Technique 15.

VI

Leadership
(continued)
Training and Retention

As one examines the current books and articles in the field of Christian education he comes to the general conclusion that the terms "leadership training" and "teacher training" are often synonymous or interchangeable. In practice, however, the term "leadership training" is usually more inclusive in scope. For example, it is used to refer to the instruction given youth sponsors, deacons, elders, trustees and other officials in the church as well as to teachers in the Christian education program. We find, therefore, that "teacher training" is generally reserved for describing those programs of instruction designed specifically for those who teach in the Sunday church school, whereas "leadership training" is a much broader term and refers not only to teachers but also to other persons seeking leadership instruction.

Need for Leadership Training

Most churches do not possess the necessary finances for "importing" leadership from the outside, nor do they in many cases desire to adopt such a policy. This implies the need for a program of training leadership *within* the church. Any pastor or minister, however, who believes he can build a program that will produce in one or two years sufficient leadership for his church is greatly deceived. Churches with well-developed programs in leadership training have found that only through hard and persistent work over a great many years have satisfactory results been obtained in this area. Institutions in the business world have discovered that only after a *long-range* program of leadership training is inaugurated and continually cultivated can they expect to produce the leaders whom they need for vacant administrative positions. God is with His church and provides it with leadership, it is true; however, even our Lord spent three long years training the Twelve in their leadership roles for building the New Testament church.

Leadership training, it must be granted, is a difficult and time-consuming task; it, nevertheless, has always been an important aspect of the church's program and continues to be of great importance in the present.

Although we traditionally think of leadership training within the church as something limited to those in active service, every training program should be planned to include not only presently engaged workers but also potential workers and any interested church members who have no apparent or immediate leadership goal in mind. In other words, we must educate church members at every level of the organization in respect to the philosophy of education and administration which is employed. Notice the importance of training for all persons and of a common outlook and philosophy for an organization:

> This rather patronizing attitude towards the subject [of training employees] has overlooked the importance of training for officials of all grades, not primarily in order that they may learn new tricks, but that, in studying methods in common, they may attain the similarity of outlook and of attack on problems which are essential to true cooperation.[1]

The education of persons at every level of the church organization will build both faith and knowledge. Knowledge will be developed in that administrative procedures and skills will be learned; faith will be developed in that an understanding of the Word of God and of the theological undergirding of the program will be acquired.

[1] Urwick, *Elements of Administration*, pp. 69-70.

Methods Employed for Training Leaders

Annual or Semi-Annual Leadership Training Programs

Any long-range planning in the Christian education program should include an annual (or semi-annual) leadership training program. If the courses are taught by capable persons, if encouragement is given to potential class members, and if accurate charts are maintained on those "in training," this can, and should, become an excellent source for church leadership. The pastor should look upon this aspect of the church's program as an opportunity for educating the church membership and its leaders. Tead has emphasized the importance of this attitude in the following words:

> In referring to the responsibility of the administrator to be himself an educator, I have in mind one dominant thought. The conduct of his work requires constant dealings with his immediate colleagues individually and in groups and occasional group dealings with other members of the working force. The sound maxim here is to make *every administrative contact one which helps to advance the learning, the understanding and the concurrence of those being dealt with.*[2]

And are not the words of Christ to His disciples applicable to His servants today to "*teach* all nations" (Matt. 28:19)? The apostles also, as James Smart has observed in his volume on the *Teaching Ministry of the Church,* carried on a teaching as well as a preaching ministry.[3]

A good teaching program for leadership development in the church should be set up to cover the important areas of study. Traditionally these areas are: (1) biblical studies, (2) theological studies, (3) studies in church history, and (4) practical studies such as evangelism, teaching methods, administration, hymnology, etc.

A church might, therefore, propose the following, or a similar, long-range program:

[2] Tead, *Art of Administration,* p. 202.
[3] James Smart, *Teaching Ministry of the Church,* p. 22.

First year .... Survey of Old Testament or
                                           Survey of the New Testament

Second year .... Survey of Christian Doctrine or
                                           The Teachings of Christ

Third year .... History of the Christian Church or
                                           History of Missions

Fourth year .... Personal Evangelism, Administration,
                                           or Methods of Teaching.

A suggested leadership program for small schools is given in Figure 10.

The leadership curriculum should be sufficiently publicized and promoted *each year* so that the membership come to see leadership training as a planned, integral part of the Christian education program.

Enlistment Interview Instruction

The enlistment interview (see p. 112) usually involves instruction in the use of materials, in the value of objectives, and the program in general. However, the learning process for the candidate or new leader does not terminate with the conclusion of the interview but, as this chapter indicates, it is only one facet of the church's over-all leadership education program. If the interview is carried through properly, it should help to create a desire for additional leadership preparation.

Annual Orientation Session

In many churches an instruction session is held for elected officers and other workers for the purpose of acquainting them with their specific responsibilities for the new year. This presents the pastor with an opportunity to outline the program, the general organization of the church, and some of the special relationships that exist between staff members and church officers. There are pastors, for example, who take this opportunity to inform church officers of their responsibility to report the need of any church members for counseling, for financial, or other types of assistance.

SUGGESTED PATTERN FOR SMALL SCHOOLS

FIRST YEAR

Methods

Foundations of Christian Teaching
211 Teaching Children
311 Guiding Youth
411 Helping Adults Learn

Enrichment

110 What It Means to Be a Christian
Life of Jesus or 124 Teachings of Jesus

SECOND YEAR

Methods

610 How to Improve the Church School
210 Understanding Children
The Methodist Youth Fellowship in the Small Church
Adult Work in the Church School

Enrichment

114 Christian Beliefs
120.2 How to Read and Study the Bible

THIRD YEAR

Methods

The Work of the Local Church
The Church in Town and Country
216 The Use of the Bible with Children
316 The Use of the Bible in Teaching Youth
416 The Use of the Bible in Adult Groups

Enrichment

The Christian and Race
113 Christian Stewardship

FOURTH YEAR

Methods

Goals and Materials for Methodist Church Schools
215 Helping Children Grow in Christian Faith
310 Understanding Youth
423 Home and Church Working Together
410 Understanding Adults

Enrichment

Prayer
History of Methodism

Figure 10. A Leadership Training Program for a Small Church. Source: *1962 Manual for Christian Workers,* The Methodist Church, p. 26.

A Saturday morning and afternoon may be devoted to this aspect of God's work, so that the result is a greater understanding of, and loyalty to, the program. The instruction period should include not only newly elected officers and those remaining on committees and boards, but also those who are the outgoing officers. In this way the orientation session can draw upon the experience of those who have already served and are familiar with the functions of their positions. The program may call for committees and boards to meet as separate groups, but join for at least one general session during the day. The church constitution, handbooks, previous plans and other materials on organization and procedure should be made available and studied carefully by all who attend.

Informal Group Training

This refers to the informal group education received by those serving on church boards and committees in regular meetings.[4] Although there are no lectures or discussions in the academic sense, yet there are many opportunities for communicating needed information to those in responsible positions. Thus, group meetings should be considered by the pastor and other staff members as favorable situations where individuals are likely to be highly motivated to learn and understand the material presented. Once potential leaders become involved in the process of solving problems they tend to accept greater responsibility because of their increased understanding of the general dynamics and circumstances.

Semi-Annual Program Planning Sessions

The general purpose of planning sessions is to outline the activities in more or less detail for the period which lies ahead. If the planning session is held several weeks before the beginning of the church year, then a full day (usually a Saturday) should be devoted to the work. At this session, plans should be set up for the following six months or entire year. It is

4 See *Infra*, p. 84.

obvious that this type of planning is essential for Christian education boards and committees if the great number of activities in the educational program are to be coordinated and given adequate support. Many Christians would be willing to give top priority to church activities if informed *far enough in advance* when they are to occur. But by the time the church announces *its* program, there have already been other activities previously planned by well-organized secular groups to which our leaders have committed themselves, thereby drawing them away on some of the most important dates of the church year. The church, then, must be satisfied with the dates which remain and with the poor attendance accompanying them. Let it be remembered that there are educational, political, social, and commercial groups all competing for the time of the average church member. Early planning, therefore, which looks to the future for six to twelve months will assure a church of adequate support and assistance in its own program. However, one can only expect conflicts and constant readjustment of dates and activities to result if advanced planning is ignored.

A well-planned program, of course, should be somewhat flexible. A practice followed by many churches is to plan the first six months of the year in greater detail than the last six months. Then at the semi-annual planning session, the groups concern themselves with filling in the details for the balance of the year. In this way they avoid a reworking of highly specific plans and devote themselves to filling in the outlines of previously projected plans.

Laboratory or Demonstration Schools

How can a Sunday church school teacher make a significant improvement in his teaching techniques? There is probably no better way than through attending a school where master teachers may be observed. Many denominational and inter-denominational agencies provide such schools at nominal cost to the individual. In churches where the budget permits, it is recommended that the expenses for regular teachers seeking to improve their teaching skills be underwritten, either in part

123

or in full. The experiences provided at these laboratory schools (where there are teachers with actual classes of pupils present) include studies in understanding students of various age levels, teaching techniques, preparation of materials for teaching, observation of master teachers, and discussion and evaluation of the sessions attended — all of which contribute most significantly to the improvement of one's teaching skills.

Community or City-Wide Leadership Schools

For the most part, these schools are designed for the training of Sunday church school teachers in a community or small town. The schools may be sponsored by a denomination's constituent churches or by an interdenominational agency. Inspirational speakers, master teachers, pastors, professors from theological schools, and outstanding directors or ministers of Christian education compose the faculties of the schools. The time which is generally considered best for church groups differs from one section of the country to the other, but the most frequent pattern for training-school sessions appears to be one offering a series of consecutive Mondays or Tuesdays running from five to ten weeks. If the courses require ten hours of classroom attendance, these hours may be divided into five sessions of two hours each, or ten sessions of one hour each. Which arrangement seems to prove the most satisfactory? From an analysis of many of the successful schools, two-hour classes held each Monday night for five weeks is the preferred arrangement. Motivation seems to remain at a high level for a five-week period, and does not diminish significantly as it does in the longer ten-week programs. It furthermore provides a more economical use of the student's time since his travel is reduced by one-half, i.e., he makes five round trips instead of ten, and only half as many evenings are required.[5]

The curriculum of a leadership training school ranges from lectures and discussions on administration, teaching methods, and

---

[5] One advantage, however, for the ten-week program is that *two* courses rather than one may be given each night — an arrangement not possible in a five-week program.

understanding students, to camping procedures, the use of curriculum materials, and the use of the Bible in teaching.

Elective Bible Courses

Because of the increased interest in Bible study, college-age and young adult classes are supplementing their Sunday church school curriculums with special studies in the Old and New Testaments. Thus over a period of time, students may receive instruction in such books as Genesis, Job, selected Psalms, in the Gospels, the book of Acts, Romans, Hebrews, and possibly Revelation. If there is included in these studies a brief survey of both the Old and New Testaments, an adult may gain sufficient confidence in his knowledge of the Scriptures so that he looks upon himself as a potential teacher or leader in the church. Thus, any investment of time and money in the education of young people and adults in the Holy Scriptures, whether in Sunday church schools or leadership training groups, will pay rich spiritual dividends to a church — with regard to biblically literate, competent, vital, and dynamic Christian leadership. And what more could a church ask!

Church Library

Teachers and leaders who are genuinely interested in serving Christ and His church at a maximum level of effectiveness will more often than not avail themselves of good reading materials. Every church should provide a theological library which includes commentaries (both critical and devotional), Bible atlases, Bible dictionaries and encyclopedias, and church history and mission texts. There should also be standard texts available in the fields of Christian education, apologetics, counseling, Christian biography, evangelism, hymnology, principles of administration, and recreational and social programming. With books in these fields available to the leaders in a church, particularly if they are made aware of the library holdings, the quality of the leadership and program should show constant improvement.

Observing Other Educational Programs

Of the many ways to encourage leaders to improve their work, perhaps one of the finest is that of sending them out to visit churches which have vital and growing programs. There are some people who cannot visualize a program in operation through hearing or reading about it. But when they can *see* a program in action, it then becomes alive and meaningful to them. It has flesh and blood, and serves, as nothing else can, to motivate them to develop and improve their own program.

A leader should be permitted to delegate his duties to a subordinate from time to time, thus enabling him to visit and analyze other programs. If he is selective of the church he plans to visit, he should return with new and creative ideas for improving his own particular area. Church members who find themselves far removed from churches with exceptionally well-developed programs might feel this to be impractical, but for those churches located within a 50-mile radius of a large metropolitan area, this type of learning experience should be seriously considered. More than one leader has been inspired by observing other highly successful leaders serving in the same field of activity.

Formal Academic Work

It is not uncommon for lay persons to enroll in Christian schools so they can prepare themselves more adequately for their church tasks. Theological seminaries, Christian colleges, Bible colleges, and Bible institutes usually make it possible for laymen to pursue studies in the areas of Biblical and Practical Theology. These studies may be offered to them in an evening school or in a regular day school. In the event that an institution of this nature is within easy traveling distance, leaders and potential leaders should be encouraged to enroll in them, because this type of instruction is especially helpful in the development of leadership attitudes and techniques.

Church Manuals

Whenever there is a high turnover in church membership, handbooks or manuals become absolutely essential for efficient church operation. Without this instructional aid, the pastor or other staff member must assume the responsibility of carrying on a program of continuous education which is monotonously repetitive due to the constant stream of new personnel, and because many people frequently forget their original instructions.

Large business corporations have avoided much repetitive instruction by issuing manuals describing the objectives, the duties and responsibilities as well as the relationships of those in the organization, and the general rules of conduct and operation. Furthermore, psychologists know that what people read they retain for a much longer period of time than what they hear. Thus a manual is superior to a lecture period for many purposes. It becomes even more valuable in that a manual can be read again and again until the instructions are indelibly impressed upon the mind of the reader. Not only does a manual, therefore, prove to be a very valuable device because it can be referred to whenever needed, but it tends to eliminate frequent and time-consuming conferences on routine matters.

Substitute Teaching

There are always some church members who, for all practical purposes, seem to be good candidates for teaching assignments. Yet, when such persons are requested to assume responsibility for a class, they decline for reasons of incompetency or inexperience. If those who fall into this category could accept teaching assignments from time to time on a purely substitute basis, they could test their skills at teaching, without fear of failing and being asked to give up a group. This could also be a means for improving whatever teaching gifts they may have so that in time both student and superintendent (as well as the teachers themselves) would feel that they had the necessary qualifications for permanent assignments.

To be assured of substitutes for this type of program, the pastor and educational director should keep themselves informed of the needs in the Christian education program and should (a) set goals for the desired number of leadership training enrollees for each year and (b) maintain charts of the leadership class registrants for future reference.

127

Retention of Church Leaders

Administrative Procedures

In the public schools, staff members are retained in large part through improvements in the educational program, improvements which include maintaining low pupil-teacher ratios in classes, providing tenure, arranging for retirement benefits, increasing salaries according to a set schedule, granting leaves of absence when needed, providing clerical assistance, and permitting vacations with pay. A perusal of these provisions quickly reveals that few if any can be employed in the typical church Christian education program where volunteers comprise the majority of the personnel. Nevertheless, there are steps which can be taken to improve the conditions under which the leaders serve and which will ultimately contribute to their retention.

One important method for retaining capable leaders involves the use of democratic procedures in the planning and direction of the program. This approach calls for the participation of all leadership personnel in the formulation of plans and decisions which will affect them. An administrator should never lose sight of each person's need "to belong" to the organization and to share in its program in a responsible way. As long as the sponsor, the teacher, or the worker has a sense of belonging to the church program, all other things being equal, he should find satisfaction in his service to the church. But as soon as he feels that rules, manuals, and procedures have created an atmosphere of impersonal relationships, he will think he is unimportant and therefore unneeded. "After all," he may say to himself, "no one seems to be interested in me or in the work that I am doing. Perhaps someone with more interest, or one who has not carried his share of the load here at the church should now assume the leadership of this group." It may be that as a member of the church he *is* carrying a much greater load than should be necessary. But it may also be that there are few, if any, who could serve any more effectively than he is in providing good leadership. If this overburdened person is to be retained, then he must be made to feel through democratic procedures that he is a genuine part of the organization, helping to make plans, sharing in decision-making, and contributing to the general program of the church.

Another administrative policy that aids in conserving leadership is one which permits a teacher to take a two- or three-week vacation in the summer, and also a week every four or five months during the September-to-June period. If a church takes the attitude that it cannot possibly arrange for five or six absences a year for a teacher or sponsor, it ought to consider the sacrifices that many Christian leaders and their families make week after week in order to promote the cause of Christ. Should it not also consider the effects upon the program if good leadership is lost and other personnel, which may be far less capable, are installed as replacements? Would it not be much better to enlist the replacement personnel for substitute service and thereby contribute to the retention of the more able leadership through a limited number of planned vacation or rest-type Sundays? We believe it would be. Many of these leaders would undoubtedly visit other educational programs on such occasions, hoping to find new ways to improve their skills and thereby strengthen their own ministry.

Retention may also be facilitated through an efficient purchasing program. Some of the best leadership in churches become discouraged when supplies do not arrive promptly and students and workers alike are forced to improvise materials at great cost of time and energy. This would be considered an "unpardonable sin" in our public schools and should be avoided in our churches through well-administered programs which schedule the purchase of supplies so that they are available at the time of need.

In short, for those in positions of administration, the attitude which ought to prevail is one of a spiritual rather than a professional concern. It ought to be that of "sharing one another's burdens," of assisting one's fellow workers who are also part of the Body of Christ. If the attitude of administrators can be positive so that it is not "how can I best recruit and retain workers for this organization and make *my* load a little lighter?" but, instead, "how can *we*, as the Body of Christ, work most effectively in the cause of Christ, in the winning of individuals to a personal commitment to Jesus Christ?" then a church with this purpose and concern will display the kind of dynamic growth which is so urgently needed today.

Instructional Procedures

With the advent of television, radio, and the book-publication explosion, students are constantly exposed to situations, real or vicarious in nature, which raise questions about the relevance of the Holy Scriptures to the problems of life. The leaders in our churches are finding it more and more difficult to answer these questions, with the result that students have often lost respect for, and interest in, the church. Teachers, especially, have felt the embarrassment of searching for answers to students' questions while standing before their classes. They are eager to avoid such situations if they can. But the only satisfactory solution is to provide teachers and leaders with subject matter that will truly prepare them for answering the questions which arise in the course of teaching. Simply stated, teachers must be able to hold the confidence and respect of their classes. They must combat the student attitude which says: "Public school teachers have the answers for our questions, why is it that our Sunday church school teachers do not?"

How *can* leaders prepare themselves for these situations? Where will the subject matter be obtained for securing the answers to student questions? Preparation should come from the church's leadership training program. In addition to the scheduled courses and other activities for training leadership, the church should invest a modest sum of money in the purchase of inexpensive study books as gifts for leaders to use and to keep for their own personal library. This will not only encourage them to study, but it will also be a means for expressing the appreciation of the church for their faithful service.

If the instructional program includes an evangelistic emphasis that has for its objective the introduction of young and old to Jesus Christ as Savior and Lord, it will inspire leaders as nothing else can. Although Timothy was acknowledged as a teacher, he nevertheless was exhorted to "do the work of an evangelist" (II Tim. 4:5). The church with an evangelistic spirit will be a church where sinful hearts, unethical practices, and despairing lives will be changed by the power of God. The Holy Spirit will be found carrying out His ministry of conforming the regenerated to the image of Jesus Christ. Christian leaders will see husbands and wives reunited, young people dedicated to God and His church, and businessmen practicing the principles of the Christian faith in their daily transactions. When teachers and leaders witness these changes they will come to realize that despite the sacrifice and endless hours of work connected with the conduct of the church's program, theirs is the most important task on earth. *Seldom does a leader resign from a program when evangelism is a vital, integral part of that program.* There is nothing that can inspire a leader to continue his work like the evidence of changed lives within his own class or group.

In summary, then, there is a twofold program for retaining teachers: good administration and an adequate instructional program which includes evangelism as one of its major emphases.

Evaluation of Leadership Ability

Need for Evaluation

Churches should evaluate, but why? There are many reasons which may be given for evaluating leadership abilities. Among these are:

(1) The interest of a leader in teaching or leading a group may be at a high level at the outset of his leadership assignment but may decrease with time until marked inefficiency results.

(2) Those who have reached an age in life when their mental and physical capacities have diminished may become ineffective, unknown to them or to those administering the program (but very much in evidence to those sitting under their leadership).

(3) In rapidly growing churches it may be discovered that those who were once acceptable as teachers or leaders of smaller groups do not possess the skills for continuing their present work with expanding groups and departments. In other words, there are some leaders who are skilled in administering or teaching smaller groups but not larger ones. If this is the case, then adjustments should be made.

(4) A final reason is that leaders may be in need of assistance

but are reluctant to seek it. In such cases, evaluation will frequently indicate this need before a condition has become too serious to remedy.

It is incumbent upon the person who does the work of evaluation, whether he be pastor, education director, or layman, to follow the principle of assisting the individual in the most profitable and expeditious use of his gifts, skills, and aptitudes. It is *not* the responsibility of the evaluator to judge or recommend dismissal; rather, it is to encourage, to guide, and to help every member of the church in his God-given ministry, however large or small. It is that of studying personalities with their related skills and then seeking to place them where they can function most effectively for God. Thus, we may transfer a person from one responsibility to another which is more suited to him, but we must not, according to biblical principles, take the attitude that he has no place in the program of God apart from being a passive listener. In the business world, every effort is made to show concern for the individual even to the extent of shifting him from one position to another in order to discover where he might best function for the good of the organization. Today the general practice, though there are always exceptions, is to find the right place for a worker, instead of dismissing him. In Christian circles, most of all, the practice of prayerfully seeking the right place for a member of the Christian community should be a duty and an obligation for those in administrative positions.

Methods of Evaluation

Some of the methods used for determining leadership ability are: verbal reports of students or group members, stenographic reports of all words spoken and activities engaged in, rating scales, tape recordings, monitoring by way of intercommunication systems, and by the results of tests taken by students.

Anyone familiar with the problem of recruiting leaders for a church program is aware that for the average church most of the methods mentioned above would be unwelcome. The church, we repeat, is a voluntary organization. Anyone who teaches or sponsors a group is doing it as a service of Christian love. If there is the slightest indication that there is dissatisfaction with a leader's performance, he may submit his resignation before the degree of his effectiveness can be ascertained. To put it realistically, the church usually lacks the leadership it needs, and any program of evaluation that would psychologically threaten a leader would probably reduce the number of leaders to a point that is damaging to the program. Even those in the business and educational world are sensitive to appraisals of their work by others. Economic necessity, however, persuades them to remain in their positions. This is not true in the church. There is no economic pressure to keep people in church positions. There must be an *internal motivation* of Christian love, not as a means but as an end, for the work which holds leaders in the program. In the light of these factors, what methods of evaluation may be used without discouraging those whose work is to be evaluated?

(1) *Leadership Questionnaire.* This is a series of questions for the purpose of self-evaluation. The questionnaire is kept by the leader so that he is the only person to know the results of the evaluation items. This is an indirect, but nevertheless, a very worthwhile method for helping the leader gain an insight into how effective he *really* is in his work. It is ideal for persons who are conscientious but who may not have reflected upon or recognized some of their inadequacies.

(2) *Informal Interview.* Usually this method of evaluation should be employed outside of a scheduled church situation. It may be over a cup of coffee in one's home or at a coffee shop. A church social affair may also serve as an opportunity for discussing such matters casually and yet sincerely.

(3) *Attendance Records.* One of the first indications of poor leadership is in a declining class or group attendance. In the public schools where attendance is compulsory, this method is obviously less suitable. But in a church situation, a decreasing membership is a general indicator of the holding power of the group's program and the leader's ability. On the other hand, an increase in attendance would be a positive indication that the teacher or leader was skillful in his work. If this measure is employed, the evaluator should focus attention on the attendance statistics — *not* on the leader. The problem becomes

clarified through the use of attendance figures, and interpersonal tensions are, or can be, minimized through their use in an objective manner.

The evaluator should be aware that many factors other than leadership ability may affect attendance. Population turnover, changing neighborhoods, military service assignments, sickness, vacation periods, weather conditions, lack of a pastor's interest in Christian education, suspension of a church visitation program, etc., may cut deeply into attendance figures. A further caution, however, is that a heavy social emphasis or other program elements might result in a marked *increase* even though the more important aspects of the program such as teaching ability, and the use of the Bible, might be of a poor quality.

4. *Departmental Tests.* Again, this is an indirect method for determining leadership effectiveness. If there is a specific amount of material to be learned, a test may be devised to examine all the students in a department to ascertain which classes obtain the highest scores. This could only be done, of course, if the classes involved had the same lesson material. For valid results from the standpoint of testing, therefore, the groups would have to be divided so that they would be equivalent in terms of educational background, intelligence, etc. But if these matters were set aside and the testing done on a very informal basis it should stimulate teaching to a greater extent. That is, teachers would be motivated to instruct their students as thoroughly as possible, so that their class scores would be above an arbitrarily chosen figure.

5. *Group Member Comments.* Although student judgments are not always reliable or as valid as those of a trained observer, they nevertheless are a helpful indication of a leader's ability. Pastors, superintendents, and educational directors should avoid using a single measure for evaluation purposes, but should supplement it with several of the other methods indicated above.

Dismissal or Transfer of Leaders

It is at the point of dismissing or transferring leaders that a great deal of Christian tact and sincerity is required. If all potential leaders could be screened by using and observing them in a substitute capacity before appointing them to a permanent position, it is quite probable that the necessity for removing individuals from leadership positions would be a rare thing indeed. But if a situation exists in which a leader must be removed from his position, every effort should be made first of all to shift him to another job and thereby avoid an actual dismissal. This is based, as we have indicated before, on the belief that every person has his part in the Body of Christ, and it therefore becomes the responsibility of the administrator or the Christian Education Board to suggest a transfer and find that position in which the member can best serve.

The procedure of asking the Board of Christian Education rather than an administrator to suggest a change in a position of leadership helps to insure that a fair decision will be rendered. This is due to the fact that not one but several individuals (members of the board) are involved in the decision. In order to avoid the charge of unfairness, therefore, a pastor or educational director should refer the consideration of leadership transfers to a board or committee with the proper constitutional powers. This generally gives greater protection to the individual concerned as well as to the one who serves in an administrative capacity. There are cases, however, of a confidential nature which should perhaps be dealt with by one or two persons, particularly if information highly embarrassing or detrimental to the individual (or to the church) is not to be disseminated to a large number of board members — and then to their families and to the church at large. Assuming that an administrator has good judgment and is fair in his decisions, this latter method is sometimes preferred, in that it keeps information of an embarrassing nature from becoming widespread. As in most cases of an administrative nature, only the judgment of the minister or educational director can determine which of the above courses of action should be taken.

Summary

In Chapters 5 and 6 we have dealt with the basic divisions of work in the leadership training program of the church, namely, the identification, enlistment, training, and retention of leaders.

In the former chapter the necessity for a proper "educational climate" for recruitment purposes was pointed out. This is created primarily through the active interest of the pastor in the ministry of teaching even to the extent of cooperating in the recruitment of leaders himself.

Assuming that leaders are available in a church, it is still highly important for a church to "fit persons to jobs" rather than to do the opposite. Therefore, every source of leadership, ranging from visitors to the church, to church officers, should be examined to make certain that qualified candidates are selected. The approach to potential candidates should be one based on the belief that all members have a responsibility and function in the Body of Christ. Every effort should be made, in view of this, to find a place of service for each church member according to his skills, abilities, and experience.

The church leadership training program involves far more than recruitment. It also involves an extensive in-service training program as well as one designed to retain capable leaders. Suggestions were made as to the types of methods presently employed for training leaders in the churches (annual planning programs, orientation sessions, church library, visiting other educational programs, church handbooks, etc.). Beyond these were emphases on democratic administrative procedures and on evangelism efforts as the *sine qua non* for successful educational programs.

References to Administrative Techniques in Appendix

1. Read Techniques 4, 5, and 12 for printed materials useful in leadership training.
2. Principles on the planning of conferences as a leadership training tool are given in Techniques 6, 7, and 19.
3. Programs of three different types for teacher training may be studied in Technique 16.

VII

Coordination

Introduction

Another of the basic functions of administration is that of coordination. This is the key to efficiency in the achievement of an organization's stated objectives. It is the means whereby much confusion and duplication of effort are materially reduced. And it is also the means whereby many conflicts, tensions, and resentments are eliminated through the integration of activities.

Coordination may be defined as the act of achieving unity and harmony of effort in the achievement of organizational goals. It is, in other words, the regulation of activities so that efficiency of operation results. In referring to this process in the business world, Tead states that coordination is the work of assuring that production, sales, finance, personnel, as well as the lesser functional activities, are integrated and interrelated, with regard to both appropriate structures and attitudes, in order to achieve as smoothly as possible the desired end result.[1] Pfiffner defines it as getting people in an organization to work together harmoniously to achieve a common goal with a minimum expenditure of effort and material.[2] It should be noted that both Tead and Pfiffner consider a chief outcome of coordination to be a smooth operation with minimal friction. Organization, as we have indicated in Chapter 2, is concerned with *setting up the structure* within which personnel work; coordination is con-

---

[1] Tead, *Art of Administration*, p. 102.
[2] Pfiffner, *Supervision of Personnel*, p. 54.

cerned with the *efficient operation of plans* within that structure so that objectives are easily attained.

> In other words, it [coordination] is the operating side of organization. Where organization is concerned with quantities and numbers and the setting up of a structure to facilitate their unified working, coordination is concerned with securing that working from day to day and hour to hour.[3]

The process of coordination, therefore, seeks to promote a program that is characterized by integration, efficiency, and general unity. For example, when we see a football or baseball team functioning smoothly, we know that there is a high degree of coordination between the players. Each player knows what the general plan of action is going to be and guides his movements and decisions accordingly. Both a proper balance and a spirit of harmony are important for the achievement of the team's goal of winning the game. This concept of a smoothly functioning team applies not only to athletic groups but to all organizations of varying types, including the church. If the programs in our churches can also be characterized by teamwork and harmony, then the greater should be their achievements and accomplishments for God.

Vertical Phase of Coordination

Coordination in either an upward or downward direction is achieved largely through the exercise of authority as one occupies a line position. The authority may be of an "organizational" type which is delegated by superiors and is recognized and accepted by subordinates at all lower levels of the organization, or it may be authority having its source in the knowledge that an individual possesses. For example, people may follow "Mr. Smith's" suggestions because of his educational background and training. This is authority through knowledge. If "Mr. Smith" possesses "organizational" authority as well, he may find few occasions in which he needs to call attention to this additional authority that has been granted him by a superior or a board. By virtue of his knowledge, he is given the right to

[3] Gulick and Urwick, *Papers on the Science of Administration*, p. 77.

exercise authority, whether it be of a formal or informal nature.

Authority of either the "organizational" or "educational-experiential" type (or both of these) is an adjunct to the initiation and implementation of plans and serves as an important means of coordination. That is, through the authority one exercises, he can assign duties to subordinates. He can tell them what is to be accomplished, how it is to be accomplished, and when it is to be accomplished. The personnel in the organization, in so far as they recognize the authority-relationships which exist, will carry out whatever assignments are given them. This is one of the reasons for constructing an organizational framework of line and staff relationships. There must be an understood organizational structure with varying degrees of authority inherent in it. Without organization, however, there can be little or no authority, and without authority there can be no coordination.

Most important to the vertical aspect of coordination is the process of communication. Church personnel must have policies and directives communicated to them if they are to know what is expected of them. A family, a church, or even a nation will soon lose all direction without established lines of communication with its own members. A properly functioning communication system, therefore, is vital to efficient operation. It facilitates the distribution of information to all in the organization so that each person will be acquainted with the activities and plans of other members and coordinate his own plans accordingly.

One of the unique situations existing in the churches and rarely found in formal business organizations is the appearance of the majority of its leaders and workers on only one or two days a week rather than on five or six. This severely limits the opportunities for face-to-face discussion of plans and problems with key personnel. The author himself found that a constellation of communicative techniques, including a church mailbox for key members, was necessary if he wished to convey in a prompt and efficient manner the essential information needed by those in the church educational program. The time available on Sundays and Wednesdays was not nearly sufficient for the purposes of interaction and communication.

The vertical aspect of organization provides for channels of communication and makes it possible to improve coordination through the use of several kinds of media. Some of the media of communication employed in two-way vertical coordination are:

1. Memoranda and letters
2. Formal reports of committees and other groups
3. Manuals of organization and procedure

In short, it may be said that the vertical phase of coordination is primarily identified with the chief characteristics of the scaler process, viz., authority and communication through the line aspect of organization.

Horizontal Phase of Coordination

When we speak of horizontal coordination, we refer to the integration and synchronization of activities between divisions or departments on the *same* organizational level. Horizontal coordination differs from that which is vertical. Those who have studied administrative theory are fully aware of the resistance that individuals oftentimes give to directions which come from higher levels of authority. Vertical coordination in such cases may be achieved through the use of authority. But how are the personnel in several departments on the same organizational level encouraged so that there is horizontal integration and *maximum* effort in the coordination of their activities without authority being available for this purpose?

James D. Mooney, former Vice-President of the General Motors Corporation, has provided us with what is perhaps one of the most commonly accepted methods for developing horizontal coordination. "In all forms of organization," he says, "what I have called horizontal coordination is the principle that *indoctrinates* every member of the group in the common purpose, and thus insures the highest collective efficiency and intelligence in the pursuit of the objective."[4] In other words, horizontal coordination may be achieved through psychological unity. Essen-

[4] *Ibid.,* p. 96.

tial to this is an integration of will and enthusiasm for the objectives and activities of a program. Efforts at coordination which lack these qualities can only lead an organization into conflict and confusion with people working at cross-purposes with each other. However, when people possess a deep sense of responsibility and *want* to attain a certain set of goals and, moreover, find that they can best accomplish these through teamwork, they are willing to put away differences for the sake of achieving their common cause.

Of course, the supreme objective, the one dominant idea that should characterize the church and create psychological unity — indeed, the thought that dominated our Lord's mission to this earth — is that of seeking men who are unreconciled to God and who are condemned by their own selfishness and sinfulness. It is the evangelistic motive of guiding others into a commitment of themselves to Jesus Christ as Lord and Savior. If this goal is held before the people continuously, it will prove to be the one inspiring and dominant idea which sets the foundation for self-coordination and ultimately for horizontal coordination.

The importance of a dominant idea such as this cannot be overestimated. It may be compared to the voluntary coordination of activities by a group of people attempting to rescue a drowning man. The danger and urgency of the situation are clearly evident; everyone cooperates so that there is maximum coordination of effort. The dominant idea is that of focusing all human effort on the objective of saving the man who is in danger of losing his life. Jesus said that He came to seek and to save the lost (Luke 19:10). And the great objective of the church should be the objective of her Lord. Seeking the lost, therefore, should be the one dominant and valid idea that surpasses all others in the achievement of coordination.

The reader may, of course, question the use of the above idea as a *means* to the achievement of coordination. Such a question would be most justified. Should we employ the concept of guiding men into a personal commitment to Jesus Christ as Lord as a means rather than as an end? To this question, the reply must be an unqualified No! Instead, this concept is *both* a means and an end as it has been described here. One could scarcely be justified in using a spiritual means for the attain-

141

ment of a material end (i.e., coordination). The destiny of souls is always more important than the achievement of organizational efficiency or any material goal irrespective of its degree of goodness. Let no administrator deceive himself: he must be sincere about, and believe in, the methods which he employs as well as the ends which he hopes to achieve. The hypocrite, whether in church or the business world, who uses inspiring concepts simply for the sake of expediency will soon be discovered. One must be true to God and true to himself, particularly in Christian work where the spiritual destinies of men hang in the balance and are influenced by the behavior of those within the membership of the church.

A factor concomitant to coordination is that of complete and thorough training. The more thoroughly a person is prepared to understand his job and how it is related to other positions in the organization, the more he will cooperate in promoting the program. If there is overlapping or duplication of duties because someone has failed to delegate responsibility with its clearly defined limits, then the coordination of the program will be difficult. A carefully planned leadership training program, however, will instruct the personnel in the responsibilities which are theirs and will outline the limits of their operation.

One very important type of training is that which provides instruction in the early stages of a plan or project. Because of the voluntary nature of church work, there is often only limited time or resources for learning the facts about a proposed program. If workers are introduced to a complex program situation at a critical point, with only minutes available for acquainting themselves with the important facts of the program, then obviously things will not proceed as smoothly and as efficiently as might be hoped. Program participants, therefore, must be introduced to the program outline in the early stages of planning. The insights which they receive in these stages will provide them with the understanding for the initiation and implementation of the program when the time for putting it into operation arrives. Early instruction, then, leads to coordination; belated instruction leads to confusion and possible chaos.

An example of poor coordination due to improper planning is that involving the typical Daily Vacation Church School conducted by most churches in the summer of each year. Those churches which begin their planning in the month of February (with the school planned for the latter part of June), continue their work through the end of May, and *then* seek out teachers, assistants, pianists, and other workers, and moreover seek to give instructions to these recruits in several hastily announced, poorly planned (and poorly attended) meetings during the month of June, will experience something very near to complete disorder and frustration. Only when personnel have been privileged to participate in the early stages of planning will they understand the curriculum and the program as they should. Coordination of both a vertical and horizontal nature under these circumstances is far more certain than in situations characterized by late planning and limited participation.

Devices Useful for Securing Coordination

Each church is unique. One church may find a device extremely useful for the coordination of its activities. Another church may discover that the same device is ineffective for its situation. But the list of coordinative devices given below should be suggestive for improving most programs at one point or another. It probably would be incorrect to say that the more devices a church employs, the more efficient it will become. It may be safely stated that a *combination* of carefully selected coordinative methods will serve to prevent confusion and keep the program in smooth operating order, more so than will a single device. This is due to the fact that people learn through reiteration. The more often a thing is repeated through a variety of methods — not through one method alone — the more likely it will be remembered. A variety of devices which have been selected as applicable to one's own church situation, therefore, should significantly improve the coordination of present and future programs.

Church Calendar

The regularly scheduled activities of the church should be listed for the year and distributed to all officers, workers, and

143

SUNDAY	MONDAY	TUESDAY	WEDNESDAY
	1 Workers' Conference — 7 PM Soft Ball League — PM	2 Weekly Staff Meeting — 9-11	Counseling 4-5 Prayer Service — 7:30 PM
7 Missionary Emphasis — AM Youth Choir—5:30 Sunday Eve Fellowship — 6:30 Topic: Social Hour—9 PM	8 S. B. L. — PM	9 W. S. M. 9-11	10 Counseling 4-5 Prayer Service — 7:30 PM
14 Youth Choir 5:30 Sunday Eve Fellowship—6:30 PM Graduation Program Topic: Social Hour—9 PM	15 S. B. L. — PM	16 W. S. M. 9-11	17 Counseling 4-5 Prayer Service — 7:30 PM
21 Lunch — 1:00 PM Visitation — 2:30 Youth Choir—5:30 Sunday Eve Fellowship—6:30 PM Topic: Social Hour—9 PM	22 S. B. L. — PM	23 W. S. M. 9-11	24 Counseling 4-5 Dinner — 6:30 Prayer Service — 7:30 PM
28 Youth Choir—5:30 Sunday Eve Fellowship—6:30 PM Social Hour—9 PM	29 S. B. L. — PM	30 W. S. M. 9-11	

Figure 11

Calendar for a Single Month for Senior High Young People.

Source: *Special Projects for Christian Education of Youth,*
Copyright by Robert K. Bower, 1959.

THURSDAY	FRIDAY	SATURDAY
4	5 H.S. Bible Club 7:00 PM	6
11	12 H.S.B.C. — 7 PM	13 Trip to Catalina —
18	19 H.S.B.C. — 7 PM	20 H.S. Graduation Banquet 7 PM
25	26 H.S.B.C. — 7 PM	27 S.S. Picnic 10:00 AM— 6:00 PM

staff members. If at all possible, the calendar should be distributed to the church as a whole. The cost of printing and distributing a calendar for the whole membership should not be prohibitive since it will tend to promote greater loyalty to the program and build up general attendance (and also church income) over a period of years. Only those with a short-range view of building an educational program will oppose the distribution of a church calendar because of the cost. A long-range view will recognize the businesslike planning incorporated in an annual church calendar and the motivation it will provide for leaders and others to plan their personal programs, with the church coming first rather than last in their thinking.

Perhaps one word of warning should be offered here. The usual church calendar which is kept in the church office for guiding the staff is not, in the author's opinion, a satisfactory substitute for a calendar which is distributed to the entire membership. Members, particularly all leaders and workers, must have in their *own personal possession* the calendar of events for the year — a calendar which they may place in their homes for constant reference.

Christian Education Planning Book

This is a book which· is used, as the name indicates, for planning purposes. One person should maintain it. The Minister of Christian Education or someone responsible to him may be approved for this task. It may also be some member of the Board of Christian Education who is given this responsibility. Whether it should be loose-leaf or permanently bound is optional. Its contents, in either case, should include educational plans of both a long-range and short-range nature, extending into the future for one, two, or even five years. It should, of course, remain in the possession of the board and be used to provide continuity for the planning of the educational program in so far as this is possible.

Written Reports

There will undoubtedly be activities planned which have not been included in the annual church calendar. If reports and

146

minutes describing projected activities are submitted to the Minister of Christian Education prior to their implementation, he will have sufficient opportunity to coordinate these with the activities already listed in the church calendar. Of course if there is any conflict, the activities scheduled in the annual church calendar should receive preferential treatment.

Organizational Chart

Elsewhere (p. 36) we have explained the values inherent in a chart that diagrams the administrative relationships between those in leadership positions. A chart of this nature should be distributed to all officers and workers to help them visualize the organization, its work, and its personnel in their various relationships. If the church distributes a manual to new members, an organizational chart should be included, thereby providing an excellent means for their orientation to the administration of the church. This becomes a coordinative device in that each person knows to whom he may go for assistance rather than moving from one office to another to seek the person with the knowledge and authority pertaining to the matter at hand.

Administrative Handbooks

This type of coordinating device should be available to all who function in a leadership capacity. Duties should be defined clearly, procedures for emergency situations explained, and other items of an essential nature should be included. Handbooks which are issued annually for specific groups may include the names, addresses and telephone numbers of officers and leaders, important activities along with their dates, constitution and by-laws, scheduled programs and projects for the year. Thus, some handbooks are rather comprehensive, covering all aspects of the church or Christian education program. Others are designed for specific areas of the program so that a number of handbooks are made available (e.g., handbooks for the Sunday church school, Sunday evening youth groups, boys' weekday church groups, girls' weekday church groups, men's fellowships, women's societies, etc.).

Weekly and Monthly Conferences

For the church staff and certain other groups, weekly meetings are absolutely necessary if activities are to be kept coordinated. But other groups may find monthly conferences adequate for their purposes. Examples of conferences which may prove useful are: Sunday Church School Teachers' and Workers' Conferences, Sunday Church School Executive Committee Meetings (consisting of superintendents and general secretaries), Church Youth Officers' Meetings (occasionally referred to as Youth Council Meetings), and Released-Time Committee Meetings.

Dominant Idea or Motto

This coordinative device has been discussed in terms of its value for achieving a sense of unity (pp. 140-41). The concept which is used should be directly related to the supreme mission of the church and be emphasized regularly through printed materials, brochures, and other communication media. Some commonly used ideas are: "Teaching to Win," "Commitment to Christ," "Faith Gives the Victory," and "Take Up Your Cross Daily."

Ex-officio Memberships

These are usually extended to persons at the upper levels of organizations so that they can gain information for coordinating the general program and for making decisions that are in the best interest of the group. A pastor, an associate pastor, a minister of Christian education, a moderator, or others may be given ex-officio privileges. This permits them to be members of certain selected committees with or without voting rights, as determined by the group or by the constitution and its bylaws.

Liaison Members

As a coordinating technique, this is rarely used in any but the largest churches. More frequently it may be used in the armed services or in large organizations — such as church denominations — which are nationwide and depend on officials who can provide information or explain new programs as a means of coordinating the work of its constituent members. The liaison person may be one who carries information from one group to another but does not possess any authority, by virtue of his position, to give directions to others.

Church Bulletins

This is perhaps the most commonly used device for coordinating church activities. It is distributed to all worshipers on Sundays and lists the activities for the coming week. The disadvantage of this method as a coordinating device is that most people today plan many of their business, educational, social, and recreational activities a month to three months in advance. By the time the church bulletin reaches them, their time is already allocated to other events. Those church bulletins which announce important events for a month ahead are doing the church members a genuine service, but even this cannot begin to compare with the more efficient method of distributing annual church calendars to the entire membership.

Church Paper

There are many churches which publish a church paper in addition to a church bulletin. This too may be employed for publicizing and coordinating activities. The problem which most churches find in producing a paper, apart from the financial aspect, is that of recruiting the necessary journalistic talent with sufficient time and dedication to produce it on a regular basis. If a paper is to be started there should be reasonable assurance that there are personnel who will continue its publication for at least a year or longer.

Delegating Responsibilities to a Single Person

Because this coordinating device has already been discussed in this volume under the subject of "unity of management" (pp. 29, 46, 90), little space is being devoted to it in this chapter. It is nevertheless one of the most important methods of

149

coordination available to the administrator. It permits him to expect from his subordinates the performance of duties assigned to them. If, however, a specific assignment is given not to a single person but to several, any failure to perform the assignment would affect coordination to a greater or lesser degree and would be difficult to attribute to any one person, thereby fixing blame for the failure on no one unless it be the administrator himself. Without the use of this coordinating device, therefore, inefficiency and general disorganization are almost certain to result.

Informal Conferences

This is one of those administrative devices which are multi-objective. The author has discussed it in the chapter on Delegation (p. 84). Its technique is that of the administrator and his subordinate meeting on a very informal basis (over cups of coffee, e.g.) to consider the progress of the general program. Through such conferences many of the hindrances to coordination can be minimized or eliminated before they pose any serious problem. Of course, many of the other methods already described should be combined with the use of this technique to assure a well-coordinated program.

Simultaneous Board Meetings

In larger churches where each individual is limited to membership on one board at a time, the various boards may decide to meet simultaneously, for instance, on a Tuesday evening. The advantages of meeting in this fashion lie in at least two directions. It first of all permits a liaison operation between boards at the same hour. Important requests may be carried from one board to the other for *immediate* action. This is far superior to the usual custom of making requests one month and waiting until the following month for their acceptance or rejection by another board or group. Another advantage is that questions requiring specific answers from other boards before further planning can be done may be handled promptly through this type of arrangement, thus avoiding needless delays.

Budget Allotments

The use of budget allotments as a coordinative technique is not often considered. Nevertheless, it is a most helpful method for reducing the number of activities of a group if such activities obstruct the coordination of the general program. This technique is of value if the activities of a group are in one way or another subsidized by the church. Thus, if a particular church group has planned too many activities for effective coordination and has done so in spite of the suggestions of the Board of Christian Education, a reduction in allotments for the ensuing year may be the only method for achieving the level of coordination that will maintain a well-ordered and well-directed program.

Church Mailbox

This device also has been previously referred to in this chapter p. 139). In the event that some box holders neglect to call for their mail, it is sent to them through the government postal service. Board members, committee chairmen, pastor, minister of Christian education, church secretary, and others are included in the group which holds the series of mailboxes especially constructed to facilitate their work.

Relation of Coordination to Morale

Administrative personnel may provide the outline of what needs to be done, but it will be the persons at the lower levels of the organization who will fill in the details. And the *way* they fill these in promotes or hinders coordination. For instance, the better the interpersonal relations are between individuals in a department, the more willing they will be to coordinate their efforts. Conversely, the worse the personal relationships are, the weaker will their efforts be toward coordination. This inner desire of personnel to cooperate is the essential core of the coordinative process. If people refuse to work together, if there is tension, bitterness, or resentment, then coordination is going to suffer. On the other hand, where there is a desire to cooperate with every person for the betterment of all concerned, and where there is mutual respect and a submerging of selfish interests, there will be high morale and an effectively coordinated program.

An atmosphere which contributes to a high level of morale and ultimately to coordination is one characterized by frank discussions of any proposed changes. With both those at the higher and lower levels of an organization discussing in advance those matters which concern them, the negative elements of criticism, distrust, and suspicion can be averted. Working out changes *with* people, soliciting their comments, talking to them individually, describing proposed changes in understandable terminology — all of these can promote a high degree of internal coordination that is so often lacking in many organizations. This implies that superiors will discuss plans, schedules, and changes with those who will be affected by them. It also implies that subordinates will seek out help and information from superiors and will keep them fully informed of present and future activities.

Administrators should also recognize the relationship of morale to *external* coordination as well as to internal coordination. No organization lives unto itself. It influences and is influenced by outside agencies of which it is an integral part. Hence, the relationships which a church has with other churches will affect coordination in one's own church. Joint ventures of a spiritual nature (e.g., leadership training schools or evangelism conferences) or of a social nature (e.g., an associational picnic sponsored by several churches) all require advance planning and close cooperation. If one church changes its plans and fails to notify the others far enough in advance, this can often result in disappointed and embittered participants and a subsequent lowering of morale in all directions. Only as Christians realize the importance of the church's mission will they accept the responsibility that is theirs to keep morale on a high level and to build a program that is effectively coordinated both inwardly and outwardly.

Effective Communication

How one communicates his ideas to others will in the final analysis determine the degree of coordination achieved. In what way can a person best convey his thoughts to others and be certain that they are understood? Especially, how should the minister give directions and information to others?

Why Some Directions Are Not Followed

If directions are not followed it is usually a lack of understanding on either the part of the person giving them or the one receiving them. Therefore, understanding is the key to good communication. It may be that the administrator is not familiar with the capacities of those to whom he gives difficult assignments. Because of their inability to understand and do the assignments given them, they may fail to perform their tasks according to the plans. Or it may be that the administrator himself does not understand sufficiently well the nature of the task with its accompanying procedures, so that he gives incomplete instructions for carrying out an assignment. Still at other times the person delegating an assignment may employ terms which are highly technical or abstract, with misunderstanding as the consequence. Beyond these matters, one may discover that though a worker possesses the necessary skills and though the task has been accurately described, the authority for carrying out the task has not been made available and again a delay or failure in the coordination of the plans will result.

How To Give Directions

Understanding the worker, the task, and the appropriate tools of language is imperative for good communication. One must also study the circumstances surrounding the issuance of directions. That is, for each set of circumstances there is a method best suited for direction-giving.

Suggestion. This method of communicating directions is generally sufficient for use with people who are experienced and fully competent. For them, they are on a "team" and only on rare occasions do they feel that a superior needs to exercise formal authority. The spirit of cooperation and mutual concern motivates them to accept suggestions as though they were directions. Thus, the administrator may say, "What do you think, Jim, about getting tomorrow's plans out today?" "Could we do

153

it?" This is a suggestion through the use of a question which permits the competent, experienced individual who presumably knows his job thoroughly to accept the suggestion or give a reason why he feels it could not be done. Under this method he retains general control of his own activities, and his freedom to plan his work is largely preserved.

Request. The use of this approach involves the use of a question but does not assume as much freedom on the part of the one asked to reply. An administrator would assume that his request would be granted if he were to say, "Bill, could you get tomorrow's plans out today for me?" Of course, if something highly unusual blocked the possibility of granting such a request, Bill is given *limited* freedom to explain why he could not carry out the request given him.

Demand. Occasionally there appears an emergency which requires immediate action. An urgent matter makes prompt action necessary. In this type of situation one may give directions or orders with no resentment on the part of experienced personnel. "Type this letter and send it Special Delivery, Air Mail, Miss Green." This would be understood by a secretary or other subordinate without any complaint. Sometimes when a person is working with young people, where the safety of human lives may be involved, a sharp demand is the only method for obtaining prompt, decisive action from them. Directions which take the form of demands are frequently given orally. The other forms of direction-giving may be communicated in writing.

Oral Versus Written Directions

When should oral directions and when should written directions be given? Oral directions are best suited for requests which: (a) are short in nature, (b) require opportunities for questions and answers. In order to check the understanding of those to whom oral directions have been given, the administrator should encourage questions and should request that those who are to carry out the directions repeat them in their own words. This will then help the administrator assess his own ability at communication, and the degree to which the directions have been understood. It is important that those carrying out assignments

154

put directions in their own terminology rather than repeating the exact words of the administrator. It is a simple matter to repeat word-for-word what someone else has said. But as soon as one is requested to formulate the ideas in a given set of instructions in his own words, he can only do this adequately if he understands the ideas — thus the insistence on the person recasting the directions in his own vocabulary.

In the oral mode of communication the speaker should be certain to speak distinctly, and avoid taxing the memories of those receiving the assignments. Long, involved and complex oral directions on how to carry responsibilities through to fulfillment should be replaced by short, simple directions. Written directions are to be preferred to oral directions when: (a) the directions are long and complex and need a detailed explanation, (b) an assignment is being delegated which grants increased authority to an individual for its implementation (this informs others of the additional authority which has been given and will prepare the way for cooperation between all concerned), and (c) the assignment consists of a number of steps which must follow a certain sequence.

Summary

Although most of the processes of administration run parallel to each other rather than in a strict one, two, three arrangement, it may be said in general that coordination follows organization, planning, delegation, and staffing. That is, there must be an organizational framework set up; there must be plans, some delegation of responsibility, and a leadership enlistment program to secure personnel for an organization before the process of coordination can occur.

The effectiveness of the coordinative techniques used will be measured by the degree of efficiency to be found in an organization. Efficiency in turn is dependent upon the unification of human efforts and work processes. This unification may be accomplished by the use of authority and communicative methods, through the vertical aspect of organization, and by the use of a dominant idea accompanied by appropriate communicative methods, through the horizontal aspect of organization.

Beyond the more formal approaches to the achievement of coordination are those related to the principles of interpersonal dynamics which, if correctly followed, will create a sense of high morale. Principles of leadership training when applied to all members of a church or organization, so that each individual understands and feels a part of the total program, will also contribute to improved coordination.

Finally, the methods used for communicating with personnel will depend upon the importance and complexity of the content to be conveyed, the education and experience of those to receive the communications, and the degree of urgency involved.

References to Administrative Techniques in Appendix

1. Examples of printed materials which promote coordination are those concerned with a definition of duties (Technique 12), worker's covenant (Technique 15), printed programs in brochure form (Technique 11), and church calendars (Technique 17).

2. Techniques 6 and 7 illustrate the use of a schedule for coordinating a planning conference.

3. Since communication is the essence of coordination, Technique 18 provides insight into some of the methods which are available for this purpose.

VIII

Control

Introduction

The final step in the administrative process is the determination of the organization's progress toward its stated objectives. Experience has shown that it is not enough to plan, organize, delegate, staff, and coordinate, when there is no systematic means for checking on each aspect of these operations. Projects may have been assigned and duties delegated, but *are* they being carried out, and to what extent? Have you ever had the experience of drawing up a set of plans, explaining them in great detail and then discovering a few minutes before the plans were to be put into operation that several of the key participants had decided to absent themselves? This is not an uncommon occurrence in church programs. It is due in large part to the average church member's lack of dedication to the ministry of the church and ultimately to the cause of Christ. Checking with key personnel in a program on a *continuous* basis is the only method for avoiding persistent absenteeism and program failures. The "checking" process to which we have been referring is known in many other circles by the term "control." In the field of education, the word "evaluation" (which includes both measurement and assessment) is the term most often used to indicate the process of determining the extent to which a program is moving toward its goals.

Definition

Control, according to Urwick, consists in "seeing that every-thing is carried out in accordance with the plan which has been adopted, the organization which has been set up, and the orders which have been given."[1] It is concerned with the performance of activities according to the plans. It is not, however, identical with the planning process but is closely related to it. As Pfiffner has indicated:

> The word *control* is coming to have a rather precise technical meaning in management terminology. It refers to the flow of *information* about the progress of operations and production and is sometimes referred to as *feedback*. That is why planning and control go together: planning sets . . . goals; control tells you how you are doing in attaining those goals.[2]

Planning therefore, divides and organizes the work; control, on the other hand, is the means of seeing that the work actually does flow smoothly and systematically through the organization, consistent with plans.[3]

In short, it is a system of methods and devices which keeps one informed as to the progress of the organization's plans.

Specific Functions

One of the major purposes of control is to see that all activities are subservient to the objectives of the organization. No single group within a church should operate as though it is independent of all other groups. Every person, every group, is part of the Body of Christ and should display cooperation so that there is a unified program which witnesses to the "oneness" that is to be found in Christ. The church, in a sense, is dependent upon its constituent bodies for its existence. But it is also true, in a much larger sense, that the individual groups within a church

[1] Luther Gulick and L. Urwick, *Papers on the Science of Administration,* p. 77.

[2] John M. Pfiffner, *The Supervision of Personnel,* p. 46.

[3] Executive Office of the President, Bureau of the Budget, "Production Planning and Control in Office Operations," Management Bulletin, October 1949, Supt. of Documents, U. S. Government Printing Office, Washington 25, D.C., p. 2.

would have no essential basis for existence were it not for the church and all that it represents. An interdependence, therefore, exists between the church as a whole and its constituent groups. In the final analysis, the groups which were brought into being by the church must adapt themselves to, indeed, must bring their lesser objectives into conformity with, the church's program and general objectives.

Control also serves as a diagnostic aid. When control is perceived as a continuous process, as it should be, it becomes a means for the identification of situations requiring corrective action. This process becomes all the more important if action is to be taken before serious consequences have resulted from inefficient or irresponsible operations. This is particularly true with respect to working with young people and new leaders. There may be reluctance on the part of such persons to ask for assistance in carrying out newly-assigned responsibilities, or it may be a lack of personal initiative in attacking the problems which confront them. Whichever the case may be, the minister or some other responsible person should provide the guidance, motivation, and needed assistance rather than allow a new leader to fail in his work. The philosophy, for example, of allowing a young people's program to fail as a means of teaching responsibility should be used rarely. Leadership studies indicate that novices may have a need for "learning how to accept failure and defeat," but experiences of this sort should come *after* success has been experienced and confidence has been developed. We must not forget that "nothing succeeds like success."

Still another function of control is to provide important data for the formulation of *future* plans. One, of course, may direct planning operations by simply focusing on the goals ahead. But if experience may be regarded as a teacher, then the lessons learned in the implementation of past and present plans should offer valuable suggestions for future planning. It may be, for example, that a revision of tentative plans is quite in order. A sensible modification of future plans, however, should be based on accurate information. Records, written reports, interviews, and personal observations — all of which are a part of control operations — help to provide such data as are needed for this purpose.

Nor should the function of improving the program be overlooked. Though some people speak of maintaining the "status quo," this is an impossibility. Either a program moves ahead, or it falls backwards. One way to assure a steadily advancing program is to initiate procedures which point toward continual improvement. Thus, properly maintained records will reveal a static attendance situation in a class to which a teacher may have been recently appointed. Under these circumstances, the administrator might suggest a training course in methods of instruction for the new teacher, if this appears to be the need, especially if all other classes seem to be showing attendance increases. Without records, however, a need of this type might not come to the attention of a Sunday school superintendent or of the minister until it is too late for any effective steps to be taken. This condition could, of course, be due to other factors. It may be that a new course of study has been recently adopted and, despite a teacher's above-average methods of instruction, the students might have failed to show interest because the curriculum content was at fault. Again, an efficient system of records would indicate the need for an attendance study in the early stages so that prompt action could be taken. A system of control, therefore, becomes an extremely valuable aid in the improvement of programs.

A final function of control to be described here is one generally associated with the use of control data for the purposes of communication, sometimes referred to as promotion or church publicity. The people within a community and the members within a church are usually interested in the statistics of an educational program whether that program be sponsored by the local public school, by a civic community center, or by a church. "What is the nature of 'Church X's' program?" citizens of the community may inquire. Members of the church may ask, "What is our church *accomplishing* in its program?" It is at this point that the information which a system of control gathers, classifies, and interprets, may be used. Some churches will publish brochures for community distribution which include the statistics and information in easy-to-interpret tables, graphs, and pictures. In so far as the data are translated into terms understandable to parents, young people, and other interested persons, they should make a favorable impression. This becomes a matter of informing one's own membership, and those within the community, of the work and effectiveness of the church's program. Statistics, we recognize, do not describe the quality and spiritual nature of a church's program. But few can deny that spiritual progress and achievements are usually, though not always, connected with an increase in membership and activities. If a Sunday school has increased in number from 250 to 350 in average attendance, it means that more individuals are receiving instruction in the Word of God. If a cup of cold water is given in the name of Christ, if anyone has been given clothing, surely statistics can reveal these things and in part at least we find the admonition of the Bible (Jas. 2:15-17) being fulfilled. Christians and non-Christians alike cannot ignore data which reveal activities designed to take the gospel to those without Christ and to alleviate, in His name, the suffering, the disease, and the sickness which may be dragging the unfortunate down into hopeless despair. If the forces of evil can compile and distribute information which is frequently false or deceptive to promote practices harmful to both body and soul, should not the church compile truthful data and distribute these in order to create good and counter the evil which confronts individuals virtually twenty-four hours of every day?

Operational Characteristics of Control

Below the level of functions, which includes objectives, diagnosis, improvement, and promotion, are the specific operations which contribute to their fulfillment. The making up of records, the communication of information through oral reports, the process of interviewing, and other activities are referred to as "operations." What characteristics should these control operations display?

(1) *Comparative Data.* In order to determine the progress of a group or program, some basis for comparison is essential. The set of goals incorporated in good plans frequently provides the basis for comparison. Thus, the future goals become the standard to which the program is compared. A second basis involves the use of data or goals derived from past and present

161

records. For example, the attendance goal in a young married couples class might be compared with the goals of previous years to see what progress has been made. Or, comparison may be carried on in connection with other classes existing at the same time, either in one's own church or in other churches. However, in order to conduct a valid comparative study, the data must be in equivalent forms. The records for each year should be in percentages, or in the average number of new members, or in some other equivalent, quantitative measure. But to use percentage one year and the average number of new members the following year, and perhaps an entirely different measure the third year, confuses matters and prevents comparison unless the data are reworked, which of course is a time-consuming task. If, on the other hand, the same methods of expressing data are used each year, then comparisons are possible, trends can easily be detected, and control, in general, be facilitated.

If a decline in giving or attendance is noticeable in respect to a particular activity or group, reasons for the decline may be sought and appropriate steps taken. But data must be in comparable form before problem areas can be identified. There are definite advantages to be found in using records with comparable data. For one thing, the use of comparable records prevents a difficult situation from arising. There is little need for arguing or debating materials which use the same statistical measures year after year. They are quite clear and understandable. Moreover, with easily interpreted records available, a leader can sit down with a youth sponsor and by *focusing attention on the records* rather than on the sponsor, more easily create an atmosphere for an informal, relaxed discussion. The objectivity connected with the use of comparable records permits an impersonal atmosphere in which the steps "*we* can take to meet the situation" may be outlined. Another distinct advantage is that a comparison of the present records with past records is often a motivating force. The desire to surpass last year's record in terms of reaching more for Christ and His church are worthy motives. Caution, however, must be followed in this respect or officers and teachers will become more interested in the goals as such than in the reason for establishing the goals, namely, that of bringing more persons under the influence of the gospel.

(2) *Quantification.* This term simply refers to the process of putting all information for control purposes down in numerical form. Verbal or descriptive reports cannot be compared easily. It is very difficult to put descriptive reports down in tabular form and draw accurate conclusions. It is far more convenient to put information into numerical or quantitative terms. Thus, summaries and condensations of activities may be easily compared from year to year if these are set up in numerical fashion. Though it is true that quantified data do not tell the entire story, these may be supplemented through the use of brief verbal, explanatory addenda. Agencies such as denominational groups, as well as interdenominational groups, have found that the quantification of data in the form of numerical counts, percentages, and the like are useful means for evaluating their programs, though these measures are usually accompanied by other evaluative techniques.

(3) *Periodic Collection of Data.* Since it is quite impossible for any minister or administrator to carry on moment-by-moment supervision, lacking omnipresence as he does, he must make checks at the crucial points in a plan. For large or very important plans, deadlines (check points) should be established. In February, for example, the superintendents for a vacation church school should be recruited, with subsequent check points in the following months on the recruitment of teachers, the selection of the curriculum, the ordering of supplies, and the orientation of teachers.

Quarterly, monthly, or weekly reports should be required from the major church groups and the minister should set aside a time to read these through or arrange for oral reports on the activities of these groups by members of the church staff.

There may be other reports which the minister or administrator may desire but the above list should be suggestive. Reports once received should be filed away for future planning and comparison of the church's progress from one year to the next.

The Administrator's Part in Control

There are some duties which cannot be shared; they are the sole responsibility of the individual. And this is as it should be, for only when each person feels and accepts his responsibility as part of the Body of Christ shall we find the work of the church moving forward with the thrust that characterized the early Christian church. The acceptance of individual responsibility toward one's church, one's fellow men, and toward God is the key to a dynamic Christianity.

Let the administrator then recognize *his* responsibility and fulfill it. This implies alertness and keenness of perception on his part in terms of personnel placement, procurement of supplies 'and equipment, the meeting of deadlines so that projects, plans, and programs are glorifying to God and honoring to the Christ who is our Savior and our Lord. This requires discipline for oneself and for others. Thus, schedules will need to be drawn up — personal schedules and individual staff schedules. Is time being wasted? Are materials arriving on time for teachers and workers? Is there inefficiency in routine procedures? Are the skills and abilities of those in the church being put to best use? These are not questions simply to be asked and then dropped. These are questions which must be *answered* in detail and in regard to every facet of the Christian education program. When the process of control has been applied to the use of personnel, time, materials, and costs, then, and only then, can one rest in the confidence that he has truly discharged his responsibility in the most effective manner.

Techniques of Control

When we work with machines and with the laws of science we find a high degree of predictability. We can predict rather accurately what is going to happen, where it is going to happen, and when it is going to happen. However, when we come to the predictability of human behavior the degree of accuracy drops most significantly. We are therefore in need of control devices. Control, when properly conducted, "forms an automatic method of ascertaining when the unpredictable human factor goes wrong."[4] Gill has emphasized the importance of control devices when he states that a planned program for the effective appraisal

---

[4] Pfiffner, *Supervision of Personnel*, p. 52.

of results, i.e., audits, inspections, statistical studies, and reports, is essential for good management.[5] The devices available to the administrator may be divided into two areas. One involves reports and the other in-process, coordinating-control techniques. That is, reports describe activities which have been *completed;* coordinating-control devices describe activities which are in *process.*[6]

Reporting is an activity in which one gives an account of some action, event or program. It is a process of oral or written communication which usually moves in an upward direction but may move in a downward direction also. Though there seems to be no distinction made between reports and records, for our purposes records will refer to devices for tabulating data and setting down statistics, whereas reports will refer to communications which *interpret* the data in the form of analysis, comparison, and relative significance.

In general, the more complete reports are, in terms of tabulation and interpretation, the more effective will the process of control be. A comprehensive program of reporting should include at least the following types of reports and records.

(1) *Attendance Records.* Depending upon the needs of a church, records of enrollment and attendance should be maintained, preferably on a weekly or monthly basis. Quarterly reports should also be kept and compared with those of previous years. This should be done for all groups included in the Christian education program.

(2) *Curriculum Records.* Although curriculum materials are usually ordered on a routine basis, it is wise to have a folder indicating the purchase order dates and the dates of arrival. This will help foster planning and help to assure the arrival of materials at the proper time.

(3) *Visitation Records.* It would be beyond the scope of this book to present a detailed description of the programs used in

[5] William A. Gill, "Survey Principles and Techniques," reprint from *Modern Management*, p. 5.

[6] It is important to distinguish between these two processes, though at points the functions overlap. For example, there is an overlap in function with coordinating-control device functions when reports include not only material on *past* events but also on *future* events.

visitation; many, however, are available which describe the steps in setting up and maintaining efficient visitation records. These should be maintained on a continuous basis with attention being given to them on at least a monthly basis.

(4) *Board and Committee Reports.* All monthly, quarterly, and annual reports of boards and committees — usually in the form of minutes, but sometimes submitted in condensed form — should be filed for future reference.

(5) *Major Christian Education Group Reports.* Included in this category are the monthly minutes of the Sunday school (and all classes numbering over 40 — the activities of which could influence general church planning), boys' and girls' weekday groups, scouts, released-time education, Sunday evening youth and adult groups, and all others which are a permanent part of the Christian education program.

(6) *Leadership Training Records.* As previously discussed in Chapter 5, records should be kept from year to year so that the names of potential and substitute teachers and leaders will be available when needed.

(7) *Planning Records.* These are records, usually in chart form, which indicate the activities projected on a quarterly, semi-annual, or annual basis. The activities are listed vertically and the months of the year across the top of the chart horizontally. At the appropriate points on the chart, deadlines are indicated for the various activities. This enables the administrator to check at a glance the activities which should receive immediate attention from the standpoint of control (this, of course, will also serve to coordinate activities). If the administrator believes that too much time is required for this, he should realize that the planning of records is an important administrative operation and that he should reserve time for such administrative duties, just as he reserves time for reading, writing, and lesson or sermon preparation. He will soon discover that *more* time is available rather than less for his other activities if control measures are employed regularly.

Budgeting Reports

For groups receiving an allotment from the budget, it may be well to keep each one informed of any marked changes to occur. For instance, quarterly reports should be circulated so that needed cutbacks in expenditures for planned activities may be made. It is at this point that control by means of budgeting becomes operational. If the income of a church exceeds predictions, activities may be expanded. However, if income is less than anticipated, then close control of activities that require church financial support must be exercised.

To those interested in the preparation and interpretation of a budget, Russell[7] has suggested that the expenditure side of the budget during the preliminary stages of its preparation should contain at least seven columns, in addition to the entries showing the items for which appropriation is asked. The headings of these columns should be as follows:

1. Budget appropriation for last year.
2. Actual expenditure last year.
3. Budget appropriation for current year, according to latest revision.
4. Present estimate of final expenditure for current year.
5. Proposed expenditure budget for next year.
6. Increase or decrease over appropriation for current year (col. 5 minus col. 3).
7. Explanations.

Russell continues: On the income side of the budget during its preliminary stages an arrangement should be used similar to that for expenditures, the column headings being as follows:[8]

1. Estimated income in budget for last year.
2. Actual income last year.
3. Estimated income in budget for current year according to latest revision.
4. Present estimate of final income for current year.
5. Estimated income in budget for next year.
6. Increase or decrease over estimate for current year (col. 5 minus col. 3).
7. Explanation.

Under column 3, one may find to his dismay that there has been an unexpected drop in income over the first six months

---

[7] John Dale Russell, *The Finance of Higher Education*, p. 86.
[8] *Ibid.*

of the current fiscal year. This would probably call for reduced expenditures and would thereby become a major factor in the control process in that a corresponding cutback in activities might be called for.

Other Control Techniques

There are many other control techniques available to the administrator. Some of these methods may serve dual purposes — usually in coordination and in control. Even an organizational chart, for example, can be used to improve control: lines of responsibility are shown, and those experiencing difficulty in the implementation of plans can immediately determine the persons to whom they should go for assistance.

Control is concerned with getting projects done. Therefore charts, handbooks, printed memoranda, and other sources of information are useful for achieving this end. In so far as certain methods communicate knowledge to people in the organization so that they understand and feel a responsibility to carry their jobs through to completion, these methods are methods of control. Thus, we also consider memo pads, personal schedules, informal conferences, ex-officio memberships, church mailboxes, and many other coordinating devices as tools of control available to the administrator.

Over and Under Control

A final word of caution may be in order at this point. It is possible to employ control measures which are excessive and unnecessary. An administrator may exercise too much control, for example, with experienced personnel who resent someone "looking over their shoulder" constantly. They may also look with disfavor on written memoranda involving unimportant or irrelevant material. On the other hand, personnel who are new to an organization appreciate help in the early stages of their service. If time and materials are to be conserved, then close supervision for the "newcomer" through various control methods is in order. But with the passing of time and the acquisition of experience by personnel, the degree of supervision and guidance required should gradually diminish. Not that it should altogether cease, for control must go on continually, but there is a decreasing measure of assistance needed as the experience and skill of personnel increase. There is, then, a polarity consisting of too little or too much control. To know when either of these extremes has been reached depends upon one's understanding of human personality, upon the nature of the work being performed, and upon environmental factors. Only good judgment based upon intelligence and experience will inform the administrator when he has moved too far toward one extreme or the other.

Summary

Perhaps the major contribution of control procedures is that of keeping all activities subservient to the major function or objective of an organization. The possibility of overextending a program beyond present and foreseeable resources must constantly be guarded against. To avoid scattering and dissipating valuable and oftentimes limited resources, the techniques of control are used to great advantage in every efficient organization. Some of the principles of control with which we have been concerned in this chapter are the following:

1. Through the use of reports an administrator may exercise control over the program of his organization.

2. Reporting or controlling should be a relatively continuous process so that the progress of the work, the needs, and personnel requirements will be known. This means that regular, periodic sampling will take place at strategic points but not necessarily at all points of a program.

3. Reports should be uniform so that comparisons may be made with ease and facility.

4. The data gathered by control procedures should be usable, i.e., relevant and applicable to the particular church situation in which one is working. Facts alone are insufficient unless they bear a direct relationship to the church program and organization.

5. Control data are useful for purposes of budgeting, planning, and coordinating as well as for evaluation of an organization's program.

169

It would be well for the reader to recognize that the skills connected with the administrative function of control — as with all of the other processes discussed in this volume — cannot become part of his executive behavior unless he is willing to *practice* in a systematic and consistent way the principles which have been presented. Urwick is right when he says that for the "common run of men and women, administrative skill is very comparable with medical skill. It is a practical art, and practice is essential to make it perfect — *much* practice."[9]

References to Administrative Techniques in Appendix

1. Observe how control is based on defined responsibilities in Techniques 12 and 15.

2. Note the function of forms (Techniques 13 and 20) and reports (Technique 19) in control operations.

[9] Urwick, *Elements of Administration*, p. 14. (Italics supplied.)

Appendix

APPLIED ADMINISTRATIVE TECHNIQUES

ONE

Relationship of General to Specific Objectives

(Derivation of Specific Objectives for an Intermediate Department from a General, Overarching Objective; from the *Curriculum Guide,* pp. 14-28.*)

The Objectives of Christian Teaching and Training

The overarching objective is to help persons become aware of God as revealed in Jesus Christ, respond to Him in a personal commitment of faith, strive to follow Him in the full meaning of Christian discipleship, live in conscious recognition of the guidance of power of the Holy Spirit, and grow toward the goal of Christian maturity. This implies:

1. *Christian Conversion* — To lead each person to a genuine experience of the forgiving and saving grace of God through Jesus Christ.

2. *Church Membership* — To guide each Christian into intelligent, active and devoted membership in a New Testament church.

3. *Christian Worship* — To help each person to make Christian worship a vital and constant part of his expanding experience.

4. *Christian Knowledge and Conviction* — To help each person to grow toward mature Christian knowledge, understanding and conviction.

5. *Christian Attitudes and Appreciation* — To assist each person in developing such Christian attitudes and appreciations that he will have a Christian approach to all of life.

6. *Christian Living* — To guide each person in developing habits and skills which promote spiritual growth and in applying Christian standards of conduct in every area of life.

7. *Christian Service* — To lead each person to invest his talents and skills in Christian service.

Intermediate Department Objectives:

I *Christian Conversion* — Our aim is to lead each unbelieving Intermediate to experience the forgiving and saving grace of God through Jesus Christ. This means helping each one:

* For complete reference see end of this section.

(1) to recognize his failure and his inability to live up to God's standard of righteousness and his consequent need of a Savior; (2) to turn from sin and commit himself to Jesus Christ, trusting Him to give complete and continuous salvation; (3) to gain, after conversion, a growing sense of assurance as to the reality of that experience and its implications with regard to the lordship of Jesus.

II *Church Membership* — Our aim is to help each Christian Intermediate to grow as an intelligent, active and devoted member of a New Testament church. This means helping each one:

(1) to unite with a church by baptism upon public profession of faith in Christ as Savior and Lord (if he has not already done so); (2) to grow in understanding and appreciation of the nature, mission, practices, and leadership of his church; (3) to grow in loyalty to his church and to endeavor to render faithful service to Christ and fellow men through the church; (4) to develop the habit of attending services regularly and of participating in the fellowship and program of the church with understanding and appreciation; (5) to give regularly and proportionately for the support of his church and its world-wide program; (6) to transfer his church membership promptly when he changes his place of residence.

III *Christian Worship* — Our aim is to help each Intermediate to make Christian worship a vital and constant part of his expanding experience. This means helping each one:

(1) to understand further the meaning of worship and to desire to engage in worship; (2) to grow in appreciation of all elements that make worship meaningful, both in worship services and in personal devotions; (3) to grow in ability to participate meaningfully in worship experiences with members of his own age group and with the church congregation; (4) to practice daily individual worship, including devotional reading of the Bible and prayer for self and others; (5) to encourage and participate in family worship experiences.

IV *Christian Knowledge and Conviction* — Our aim is to help each Intermediate grow in Christian knowledge and conviction. This means helping each one:

1. With respect to the Bible — (1) to accept the Bible as a

way by which God speaks to him and as the final authority in all matters of faith and conduct; (2) to understand something of the origin of the Bible and of God's use of man in writing, preserving, and translating it; (3) to grow in understanding of the contents of the Bible and of the customs, geography, and history out of which the Bible came; (4) to acquire a growing comprehension of how the Bible truths apply to personal daily living and to community and world problems; (5) to commit choice passages to memory.

2. With respect to the great realities of the Christian faith — (1) to grow in his concept of the reality and nature of God as a personal loving Father; (2) to grow in his understanding of God and man, sin and salvation, and the Christion's life and work; (3) to develop a growing conviction about the truth and finality of the Christian faith.

3. With respect to the Christian movement — (1) to learn some of the outstanding facts of Christian history; (2) to become acquainted with some of the outstanding facts about other Christian groups and our common heritage with them; (3) to become aware of present-day trends and issues in the Christian movement and to realize that they hold meaning for his own life as well as for the cause of Christ.

4. With respect to this church and denomination — (1) to grow in understanding distinctive features of doctrine and polity and to develop growing convictions as to their soundness; (2) to add to his knowledge of the history, organization, program, problems and needs of the church and to develop an increasing sense of responsibility for the work of his denomination.

V *Christian Attitudes and Appreciations* — Our aim is to help each Intermediate develop Christian attitudes and appreciations in every area of his experience. This means helping each one:

1. Regarding God — (1) to love and trust the heavenly Father, Jesus Christ as Lord and Savior, and the Holy Spirit as ever-present Counselor and Source of power; (2) to revere God, respect His commands, and seek to know and do His will; (3) to develop a sense of gratitude to God for all His goodness.

2. Regarding the meaning of existence — (1) to regard all existence as the expression of God's creative power, wisdom and goodness; (2) to feel secure in the knowledge that this is God's world and that God's purposes are being worked out in it; (3) to realize that a person created in the image of God is of infinite worth, has marvelous possibilities, and possesses spiritual needs which only God can supply.

3. Regarding self — (1) to recognize his body, mind, and total personality as gifts from God to be cared for, developed, and used for God's glory and the good of others; (2) to have as his personal ideal the attainment of a mature Christian personality; (3) to evaluate his talents as he considers his future vocation; (4) to realize that he stands in constant need of God's forgiveness and help.

4. Regarding others — (1) to acquire a sense of kinship with every other person in the world and to cultivate an attitude of unselfish devotion to the welfare of people of all cultures, races and social levels; (2) to cultivate the desire to apply Christian principles in relationships within the family, at church, at school, and in the community; (3) to feel a concern for the salvation of others, and to accept the obligation to help give the gospel to the world; (4) to develop wholesome attitudes toward persons of the opposite sex in his peer group.

5. Regarding the Bible and divine institutions — (1) to develop a growing love for the Bible and an appreciation of its teachings as guides for daily living; (2) to develop a growing appreciation of the purpose for which Christ founded the church and an increasing concern for its life and work; (3) to develop an increasing love and appreciation of his home and feel a growing obligation to contribute to the happiness and well-being of his family; (4) to develop increasing loyalty to the ideal of personal purity, looking toward marriage and family life; (5) to regard Sunday as the Lord's Day to be used to honor the risen Christ; (6) to respect the ordinances of baptism and the Lord's Supper as means of honoring Christ; (7) to respect civil government and to feel the obligations of good citizenship as set forth in principle in the New Testament.

6. Regarding the present world — (1) to feel that the world as God made it is good and that all the resources of

nature and the necessity to work are gifts of God designed for the enrichment of life; (2) to recognize the many manifestations of evil in the world and to resolve to live a life dedicated to God, to resist the appeal of evil in one's life, and to be a positive force for morality and justice; (3) to feel a deepening sense of responsibility for the improvement of moral and social conditions in his community.

VI *Christian Living* — Our aim is to guide each Intermediate in learning skills and in developing habits which promote personal spiritual growth and Christian conduct. This means helping each one: (1) to grow in consciousness of the living Christ as the Lord of his life; (2) to accept with confidence the Bible and the Holy Spirit as guides in making the best use of his life; (3) to grow in understanding of why to pray and how to pray; (4) to seek to pattern all personal conduct in accordance with the teachings, spirit, and example of Jesus; (5) to strive to be Christlike in attitudes toward and relationships with his parents and other members of his family; (6) to continue to make progress in developing Christian character which will express itself in all his relationships.

VII *Christian Service* — Our aim is to lead each Intermediate to seek to make his maximum contribution to the cause of Christ. This means helping each one:
(1) to dedicate his talents to God and to develop skills in Christian service; (2) to seek God's will for his life and to begin to prepare for a vocation in keeping with that will; (3) to witness faithfully to his Christian faith and to seek to win others to Jesus Christ; (4) to appreciate and take advantage of the training and service opportunities offered him in his church program; (5) to learn to work unselfishly on a team by filling well the places of service in his church to his ability and stage of development; (6) to be a good steward of his money as an expression of his gratitude to God and as a means of supporting his church in its world missions program; (7) to show compassion for persons in need; (8) to participate in group and community service projects which contribute to social welfare; (9) to accept the ideal of self-giving service as the true goal of life.[1]

[1] Adapted from *The Curriculum Guide*, edited by Clifton J. Allen and W. L. Howse, pp. 14, 15, 25, 28.

TWO

Teaching and Organizational Objectives for a Church College Department

(College Department Teaching and Organizational Aims, First Presbyterian Church, Hollywood, California.)

Teaching Aims for Members

1. To present Christ in a clear, intelligent and vital manner as the only answer to their deepest desires.

2. To present Christ as the one who demands absolute authority over their lives — and who has a plan for each person.

3. To instill a greater understanding of the most vital aspects of Christian truth.

4. To make the gospel plain for the sake of visitors.

5. To give them a reason for their faith, that their minds as well as their hearts may have confidence.

6. To hold before them the thrilling challenge of a life lived for Christ.

7. To quicken them of their obligation to take the gospel to every man.

8. To show them the various social, moral, and international needs of the world, and how Christ can meet these needs.

9. To create a sense of fellowship and camaraderie in them for each other.

10. To instruct them in the living of the victorious, Christian life — ethics, prayer, faith, etc.

Organizational Aims

1. To establish an organization that will best fulfill "teaching aims."

2. Adequate records of all members, visitors, etc.

3. Dynamic and careful follow-up on all visitors with the aim to win them for Christ, and to put them to work.

4. Spiritual and enthusiastic check made of all members — we mustn't lose one member.

5. Organization: Must be good enough for all who want to work.
   Must develop their talents for God.
   Must use them — or lose them.

6. All activities must be planned to train leaders.

7. Use organization as a means to spiritual growth.

8. Create small fellowship groups.

9. Insure maximum evangelism and witness.

THREE

Criteria for Curriculum Selection

(Planning the Church Educational Curriculum Involves a Knowledge of Good Curriculum Characteristics; from *A Guide for Curriculum in Christian Education,* pp. 44-49.) *

COMPREHENSIVENESS

In determining whether the curriculum has comprehensiveness, the following factors will be taken into consideration:

1. The curriculum should give adequate attention to every aspect of Christian teaching which should be considered by each age group.

2. The curriculum should cover the areas of experience basic and common to each age group. Since individuals must live as Christians in several areas of life at once, the experiences of home, community, school, vocation, recreation, and many others must be presented in the curriculum.

3. The curriculum will give attention to the objectives of Christian education for each age group.

4. The curriculum will include all the areas of Bible knowledge which have particular significance and teaching value for each age group. A well-rounded curriculum of Christian education is anchored in the Bible at every point. The widest range of content must be comprehended in order that the biblical insights and resources shall have a chance to inform and guide Christian people in their total experience.

    The list which follows indicates more specifically some areas of content which a good curriculum will include. It should be clearly understood that these elements do not carry equal weight in any total curriculum or in any specific phase of the curriculum. Moreover, in any adequate curriculum, all of these concerns will be woven together in an integrated whole. This list serves only to illustrate how many and varied are the areas within the purview of the curriculum of Christian education.

---

* For complete reference see end of this section.

a. The Bible

    (1) Origin and nature of the Bible

    (2) Old Testament

    (3) New Testament

    (4) Methods of study, devotional use, and how to teach the Bible

b. Faith or Beliefs — regarding:

    (1) God

    (2) Jesus Christ

    (3) Nature of man

    (4) Meaning of the church

    (5) Bible as source book of faith

    (6) Christianity and competing world philosophies

    (7) Christian interpretation of the universe

c. Personal Experiences in Christian Living — such as:

    (1) Worship — personal and corporate

    (2) Health — mental and physical

    (3) Stewardship

    (4) Personal evangelism

    (5) Leisure time and recreation

    (6) Vocation — Christian approach and preparation, also challenge to church vocations

    (7) Friendship

    (8) Educational and cultural development

d. Christian Family

    (1) Christian interpretation of sex

    (2) Preparation for marriage

    (3) Establishing Christian homes

    (4) Parenthood

    (5) Christian relationships in the home

    (6) Families in relation to the community

e. Church Life and Outreach

    (1) Church history

    (2) Nature and program of the church

    (3) Church membership

    (4) Service in and through the church

    (5) Missionary outreach

f. Social Problems

    (1) Amusements

(2) Liquor and other narcotics, gambling, delinquency, and crime

(3) Race, group, and interfaith relations

(4) Christian principles in relation to community life, the economic order, policies of business and labor, government, education, citizenship, and world order

g. World Relations

(1) Opportunities

(2) World missions

(3) World citizenship

(4) Ecumenical movement

h. Service and Christian Leadership

(1) Opportunities

(2) Measures of preparation

(3) Principles and objectives

(4) Skills and methods

BALANCE

A good curriculum not only includes every area of experience important to each age group and all aspects of the Christian gospel pertinent in these areas, but it also carefully determines how much time should be given to each element. The following principles will enter into the decisions made:

1. The number of sessions assigned to each element and emphasis will reflect the importance of each judged in the light of other elements. For example, a larger number of sessions will be devoted to the life and teachings of Jesus than to the study of recreation.

2. The importance of each element will be judged in the light of its most effective contribution to the development of Christian personality, and in the light of its importance in the Christian faith.

3. The time assigned to any given emphasis will be consistent with the material available to support and enrich that area of interest.

4. The length of time assigned to any element will be determined by the time needed to initiate and carry through an effective experience.

SEQUENCE

A good curriculum will of necessity involve some carefully thought through form of organization. This may be in terms of over-all themes for certain periods of time or in connection with units or courses effectively arranged. A satisfactory curriculum does not consist of a mere collection of units or courses. Fragmentation is avoided and adequacy secured through careful interrelatedness of each part in the achievement of the total plan. Therefore, considerable care will be given to the placing of the various elements in the sequence that will contribute most to the development of Christian faith and character.

1. Some progression must be assumed on the part of the learner and teacher, so it is not necessary to repeat everything at every stage. There will be an apparent progression through the year and through the later years in the planning of content and experience.

2. The timing of emphases will utilize seasonal interests to the best advantage. A study on church membership, important at any time, would gain by being placed preceding Easter, when the interest of the whole church is especially directed to commitment to Christ.

3. The placement of units or courses will observe the need for variety and freshness of approach.

4. Closely related areas of curriculum will be so placed as to make use of the possibilities of cumulative learning.

5. There will be frequent cumulative learning, providing incentive to commitment and action consistent with the development level of each age group.

It is apparent from this consideration of the importance of comprehensiveness, balance, and sequence in a good curriculum that there is not enough time in the average church school to do the job adequately. This would mean that the curriculum would probably take into consideration the home, weekday school, vacation school, and other agencies of Christian education in order to provide additional time.[1]

---

[1] Adapted from *A Guide for Curriculum in Christian Education*, prepared by the Special Committee on the Curriculum Guide Division of Christian Education, National Council of Churches of Christ in the U.S.A., Chicago, Illinois, 1955, pp. 44-49.

FOUR

Rules and Policies of a Christian Education Committee

(Rules and. Policies of the Committee on Sunday School and Young People's Societies, First Presbyterian Church, Hollywood, California.)

CHRISTIAN EDUCATION DEPARTMENT

The teaching task of the church is constitutionally under the guidance and authority of the Session. This body sees fit to allocate and assign this educational guidance for the COMMITTEE ON SUNDAY SCHOOL AND YOUNG PEOPLE'S SOCIETIES, appointed by the Pastor, annually, with Session approval. The Pastor, Director, Assistant Director and Co-ordinator of Christian Education, Chairman of Christian Education Council and Superintendent of the Sunday School are ex-officio members of this committee and should be present at its sessions.

This Committee shall meet regularly at the call of the Superintendent.

This Committee shall have the following duties:

The shaping of the educational policies of the church and church school.

The choosing and approval of all study materials used in the educational processes of the church.

The shaping and approval of all educational organizations and the assignment of its leaders.

The selection and appointment of educational and church school principals and teachers as well as officials.

The careful planning for and attendance at such summer conferences as they shall approve and establishment and carrying out of such policies regarding the same, as they deem wise.

Making available teachers' training courses and helpful literature.

General counseling and guidance for the Director and the Pastors in their educational tasks.

All young people's groups must be in charge of a staff member or sponsor appointed by the staff member in charge of the

184

group involved. It is their responsibility to guard the conduct of the group and the usage of the church property.

Annual survey and approval of all benevolence budgets of the various educational groups. These benevolent enterprises shall be referred to the Session for approval annually.

The setting up and approval of the church calendar of the educational activities: i.e., graduations, special programs, awards, contests, conventions, courses, communicants' classes, decision days, etc.

For hymnals, etc., see "Music Committee" policies.

The forming and the approval of the educational department budget and the presentation of the same to the Board of Directors annually.

The allocation of specific duties to members of the church staff as the program warrants, after careful consultation with other departments or heads.

The formation of all new educational organizations, clubs or groups shall be authorized by this Committee; it shall also determine the dissolution of any group.

No delegation, individual or group shall go out in the name of, or represent this church, without approval of the Committee.

FIVE

Standing Policies of a Young People's Society

(Standing policies of the Christian Endeavor Society, San Gabriel Union Church, San Gabriel, California.)

In response to many requests for information about our uniform practices and because of the change in officer personnel each six months, the following policies have been reduced to writing. We recognize that this does not meet all the contingencies and obviously in many cases matters will need to be discussed with the Christian Endeavor Superintendent.

1. *Social events* — All *dates* and *places* for C. E. events should be cleared through the Secretary in the C. E. office, to avoid conflicts. Reservations for the use of the lower auditorium at any time should be made in the same manner.

2. *Kitchen* — Dates for the use of either kitchen should be cleared through C. E. Secretary. Arrangements should be made through the church office as to keys for the church, kitchen, silverware. A check list should be obtained in the office for detailed arrangements. The adult leaders for C.E., Primary through Young People's Departments are responsible to see that all facilities are left clean and orderly. For adult C.E. groups, the Social Chairman and President are responsible.

3. *Supplies* — All standard C. E. supplies should be secured through the Secretary in the C. E. office, located in the Youth Director's office. Requests for anything, except standard supplies, should be given in writing to the C. E. Superintendent.

4. *Prizes and Awards* — Before arrangements are made for awards, prizes, gifts of appreciation or recognition, approval must be secured from the C. E. Superintendent. This is necessary in maintaining a well-balanced program.

5. *Equipment* — A typewriter is available to all C. E. Societies when needed. Arrangements for its use should be made through the church office.

6. *Elections* — The nominating committee for each C. E. Society should be appointed by the second Sunday in April. Said committee should have a slate of names to submit to the Board of Deacons for approval on the first Tuesday in May. All Presidents and Vice-Presidents of societies at the high school

186

level and above must be members in good standing of San Gabriel Union Church. The C. E. Superintendent will see that all societies have their approved lists returned by the Sunday after the Deacon's meeting. Then the nominating committees may approach said members for the confirmation of their acceptance of the nomination. The election of nominees must be held by the last Sunday in May. Installation of officers should be held semi-annually on the first Sunday in June and December. For the installation in December, the Nominating Committee shall be appointed by the second Sunday in October. Names may be approved by the Deacons the first Tuesday in November for the election by the last Sunday in November.

7. *Promotion* — Promotion will take place once a year early in the month of June. C. E. promotion is to coincide with the over-all church program.

8. *Speakers* — In view of the fact that Christian Endeavor is for the purpose of training leaders, not more than one speaker from outside the society should be used during each three-month period. This also includes members of the church staff and use of films. All outside speakers must be cleared through the C. E. Superintendent in *advance* to avoid duplication. Remuneration for special speakers, at any meeting or social event, must be approved by the C. E. Superintendent. This is necessary as speakers are often used in more than one meeting in the church.

9. *Offerings* — Societies are encouraged as much as possible to take care of their own expense for parties, singspirations, and other social events. But when it is necessary for financial assistance, a request should be made to the C. E. Superintendent well in advance of the event and should include an estimate of the anticipated expense. This is to insure remuneration after the event has taken place.

SIX

Planning Conference Program and Schedule

(Junior High Planning Conference Program Guide, Christian Education of Youth Workbook, Fuller Theological Seminary, 1960.)

   I Purpose: The basic purpose is to plan out the year's activities for the Junior High Department. An important secondary purpose is Christian fellowship and a sense of participation in the running of the group.

  II Who's Involved? The whole Junior High Department including the officers, sponsors, teachers, and also the pastor and/or Christian Education Director.

 III Where? It should probably be held away from the church, preferably at a denominational camp or conference grounds.

 IV When? It is recommended that this conference be held quarterly, but it can be effective if held semi-annually or even annually. This conference should take place on a weekend if an annual conference, covering either Friday evening to Saturday evening, or Friday evening to Sunday noon. Quarterly conferences may be one day.

  V Areas of Planning:
     A. Sunday night young people's programs.
     B. Sings and other social times.
     C. Wednesday night Bible study and prayer meetings.
     D. Methods of publicity.
     E. Methods and areas of training.

 VI Staff Needed:
     A. Counselor for every 8-10 young people.
     B. Nurse.
     C. Kitchen crew (cooks, chef, servers, etc.).
     D. Dean and Recreation Director.

Note: Depending on the size of the conference, there may be an overlapping of duties. Qualified personnel are available in most middle to large-size churches.

VII Typical Cost: $8-$12 (may be subsidized; may utilize free-will offerings; executive officers of the group may be allowed to go free).

VIII Typical Program:

Friday evening	Leave Church	6:00	p.m.
	Arrive Camp	8:00	
	Fun Time	8:00	
	Snack	9:00	
	Devotions	9:30	
	Lights out	10:00	
Saturday	Rise	6:00	a.m.
	Breakfast	7:00	
	Planning Time		
	(e.g. socials)	8:00	
	Break	8:50	
	Planning Time	9:00	
	Recreation or		
	Free Time	9:50	
	Planning Time	11:00	
	Break	11:50	
	Lunch	12:00	noon
	Recreation and/or		
	Free Time	1:00	p.m.
	Officers' Meeting (Executive Committee meeting for formulating policy and evaluating planning times)	4:00	
	Dinner	6:00	p.m.
	Social or		
	Evening Meeting	7:30	
	Lights out and		
	Devotions	10:30	
Sunday	Rise	6:30	a.m.
	Breakfast	7:30	
	Clean up	8:30	
	Sunday School	9:30	
	Church	11:00	
	Lunch	12:00	noon
	Leave	after lunch	

IX How to Plan:

A. The three months following your conference should be planned in detail.

B. Long-range planning: The whole year should tentatively and sketchily be planned out. To give you an idea of some areas and things to plan for, the following is submitted:

1. Winter (January-March)
   Easter included.
   Plan for things requiring a long pull.
   a. Stewardship (life, money, prayer, service)
   b. Six months of definite missionary instruction
   c. Work on building attendance and membership
   d. Stress friendship and social life (snow party, Valentine's Day, Lincoln's Birthday, Washington's Birthday)

2. Spring (April-June)
   a. Retreats
   b. Graduation
   c. Summer months planning in detail

3. Summer: "Vacation Time" (July-September)
   a. Camps, conferences
   b. Emphasis on visitors
   c. Reports from those who are away for vacation time
   d. Plan for vacation time for sponsors and teachers

4. Fall (October-December)
   (Rally Day, Thanksgiving, Christmas, etc.)
   a. Yearly evaluation
   b. Rally day
   c. Homecoming and fall get-togethers
   d. Thanksgiving
   e. Christmas banquets and parties
   f. Yuletide program
   g. Spiritual significance of Christmas
   h. Missionary emphasis
   i. Youth budget

5. Make a year's calendar

6. Determine the functions of the Department
   a. Bible-teaching agency

b. Employment agency
c. Out-reaching agency
d. Soul-winning agency
e. Training agency
f. Financing agency
g. Social agency

7. Make the Department an integral part of the whole church:
   a. In membership
   b. In program
   c. In giving
   d. In service

X The Planning Conference can, and if allowed to, will, be a good opportunity to evaluate the program of the past year. Plan for a "gripe session."

SEVEN

Planning Retreat Schedule for Young People's Society

(Yearly Meeting of Friends of Southern California, Christian Endeavor Fall Leadership Retreat.)

Retreat Schedule

Friday evening

5:00	—	Registration
7:00	—	Dinner
8:00	—	Get-Aquainted Time
9:00	—	Keynote Address
10:00	—	Campfire Sharing Time

Saturday

7:30	—	Breakfast and Breakfast Devotions
8:15	—	Individual Quiet Time
8:35	—	Meet in C. E. Groups to Discuss Questions Pertaining to Yearly Meeting C. E.
9:05	—	Idea Clinic on Yearly Meeting C. E.
10:05	—	Break
10:30	—	"How To Be a Leader" Session for Everybody
11:15	—	Area Workshops*
12:15	—	Lunch
1:30	—	Afternoon Recreation
4:00	—	Area Workshops No. 2
5:00	—	"Plan-Your-Own-Program" Evaluation Questionnaire to Assist in Local-Group Planning
5:30	—	Dinner
7:00	—	One and One-half Hour Session for Planning With Individual Groups**
8:45	—	Evening Challenge
10:00	—	Marshmallow Roast Around Fire.

* Workshops in Following Areas:
    The Sponsor's Task
    The President's task
    C. E. Programing (Program Chairmen)
    Socials
    The C. E. Treasury
    Publicity
    C. E. Outreach (Look-out Chairmen)

Sunday

8:00	—	Breakfast
8:45	—	Quiet Time
9:10	—	Individual C. E. Planning Sessions**
10:30	—	An "Each-Group Sharing" of Future Plans
11:15	—	Morning Worship
12:15	—	Dinner

**Times for individual C. E. executives to get together and sketch out plans for the fall and winter program.

EIGHT

College-Age Sunday Evening Fellowship Program

(Christian Companionship Club [Ages 18-28], Moody Church, Chicago, Illinois.)

February

3　C.C. Club Retreat
　　Rose Lane Lodge, Lake Geneva
10　"This We Believe," Part I,
　　"The Inspiration of Scripture"
17　"This We Believe," Part II,
　　"The Trinity"
24　"Family Sing"

March

3　"Conducting a Service"
10　"This We Believe," Part III,
　　"Eternal Security"
17　Film — "Angel in Ebony"
　　(Combined with Youth Groups)
24　"This We Believe," Part IV,
　　"The Ordinances of Baptism and the Lord's Supper"
31　Bible Study — Hebrews 12

April

7　"The Preparation of a Message"
14　"The Missionary Candidate —Qualifications and Procedure"
21　"The First Six Months of Missionary Training on the Field"
28　"The Missionary's First Term — Trials, Problems, and Victories"

—Adapted from a
program brochure.

NINE

Summer Social Program for Junior High School Students

(Junior High School Summer Activities, San Gabriel Union Church, San Gabriel, California.)

Date	Time	Activity	Place	Cost
June 15	3-9:30 p.m.	Knott's Berry Farm		Spending money only
June 18-29	9-11:30 a.m.	Junior High Club (VBS) (Swim meet and Disneyland will highlight club activities)	Church	
July 5	1-9:30 p.m.	Beach	Huntington	$1.00
July 12	1-9:30 p.m.	A Lark at the Park	Irvine Park	.50
July 19	1-9:30 p.m.	Day in Industry (Swim, Eats)		
July 26	4-9:30 p.m.	Progressive Dinner on Bikes		.50
July 31	7:30-9:30 p.m.	Backyard Bible Study (Watermelon)	Smith's	
Aug. 1	7:30-9:30	Backyard Bible Study (Swim, Hamburgers, Banana Splits)	Green's	.50
Aug. 2	4-9:30	Backyard Bible Study (Shortcake)	Jones'	
Aug. 9	11-7:30 p.m.	Beach	Newport Dunes	.75
Aug. 16	1-9:30 p.m.	BBQ & Swim (Surprise Tour)	Brown's	.50
Aug. 18	LEAVE FOR CAMP			
Aug. 30	1-9:30 p.m.	Pacific Ocean Park		1.60
Sept. 6	11-7:30 p.m.	Beach	Huntington	

195

TEN

Planning Vacation Church School

(Planning for Your Vacation Church School, *Vacation Church School Handbook*, Department of Children's Work, Board of Education and Publication, American Baptist Convention.)

Calendar of Step-by-Step Procedures

January

1. *Set the dates for your school.* Clear community activities and plan your school for a period when children are free from other scheduled programs.
2. *Secure the director for your school* — the pastor or a leading children's worker in your church. The director is the key leader.

February

1. *Secure department superintendents.* Whenever possible use for leaders in the vacation church school those who work with the children in the Sunday church school. In any case, secure the best possible leaders of children to serve as department superintendents.
2. *Select the course of study for the year.*

March

1. *Secure all needed helpers.*
2. *Secure the vacation church school teaching materials for all workers*, and put into the hands of the department superintendents for their immediate study.
3. *Director and department superintendents meet to make plans* for training workers.

April and May

1. *Place the texts in the hands of all workers.*
2. *Train workers.*[1]

---

[1] *Vacation Church School Handbook*, Department of Children's Work, Board of Education and Publication, American Baptist Convention, Philadelphia, 1954, p. 3.

ELEVEN

Church Youth Program

(Junior High and Senior High Programs, First Evangelical Free Church, Rockford, Illinois.)

Junior High

Sunday School 9:29 A.M.
The fall topics will be:
7th grade — The Christian Life
Teachers: ——— ———
8th grade — The Word of God
Teachers: ——— ———
9th grade — God's Plan of the Ages
Teachers: ——— ———

Sunday Youth Hour 5:00 P.M.

Sept. 21 — Crusaders for Christ
Sept. 28 — Teenage Topics — "First Dates"
Oct. 5 — Bible
Oct. 12 — Stewardship
Oct. 19 — Film, "Our Bible, How It came to Us"
Oct. 26 — News from the Field
Nov. 2 — Teenage Topics, "Whom Do I Date?"
Nov. 9 — No Word from God
Nov. 16 — Seeing Straight
Nov. 23 — Thanksgiving film
Nov. 30 — Find 'em — If you Can
Dec. 7 — Palermo Bros. Combined program
Dec. 14 — You Were There — Time Machine
Dec. 21 — No meeting (S.S. Program)

Senior High

Sunday School 9:29 A.M.
The fall topics will be:
10th grade — Highlights of Scripture
Teachers: ——— ———
11th grade — Scripture Panorama Series
Teachers: ——— ———
12th grade — Foundation Series, God the Father and His Son
Teachers: ——— ———

Sunday Youth Hour 5:00 P.M.

Sept. 21 — The Kick-off
Sept. 28 — Teen-age Topics — "Going Steady"
Oct. 5 — Leonard Lovdahl, Author
Oct. 12 — What Is Your Life? Group program
Oct. 19 — Film, "Our Bible, How It Came To Us"
Oct. 26 — Christian Maturity
Nov. 2 — Your Town 1976, Group Program
Nov. 9 — Teenage Topics, "Falling in Love"
Nov. 16 — Record Roundup
Nov. 23 — Film, "The House That Hunter Built"
Nov. 30 — Wheaton College Football Gospel Team
Dec. 7 — Palermo Bros. Combined Program

Dec. 28 — Teenage Topics — "Dating Standards" Counselors: ——— ———

Dec. 14 — Teens Look at Missions
Dec. 21 — No Program (S.S. Program)
Dec. 28 — Film "Buttonwood Inn"
Counselors: ——— ———

Weekday Activities

Socials — Oct. 11, Wheaton-Elmhurst Football Game — Nov. 8, Family Recreation Night — Dec. 19, Christmas Party at Y Lodge

Weekday Activities

Socials — Oct. 11, Wheaton-Elmhurst Football Game — Nov. 8, Family Recreation Night — Dec. 13, Christmas Caroling

Band

Tues. 7 P.M.

Band

Tues. 7 P. M.

Confirmation

Sat. 10:30 A.M. with Pastor for 7th graders

Power Hour

Bible study and prayer, Wednesday 7:45

Athletics

Booster Basketball League, begins November

Adapted from church brochure.

TWELVE

Job Analysis of Church School Personnel

(Organization and Personnel of the Church School, Handbook of Bay Shore Community Church, Long Beach, California.)

Church School Superintendent

The responsibility and authority for the direction of the Church School is delegated to the Church School Superintendent, who is directly under the supervision of the Minister of Christian Education. The specific responsibilities of the Superintendent are the following:

1. To see that the personnel of the Church School are aware of the educational philosophy, objectives, plans, policies, and standards of the Church School and that these are carried out.

2. To see that all staff and teaching positions are filled by persons who are adequately trained and/or are receiving in-service guidance.

3. To see that department superintendents and teachers are familiar with the curriculum and are teaching in accordance with its general outline and objectives.

4. To stimulate and co-ordinate out-of-the-classroom activities.

5. To see that the superintendents and teachers are aware of the instructional services available and to be alert to ways that these services may be improved and expanded.

6. To see that Church School personnel properly appreciate the importance of the home-and-church program and that they are using every opportunity to promote and participate in the program.

7. To see that adequate publicity is given to the work and objectives of the Church School, particularly for parents of Church School members.

8. To report to the Minister of Christian Education parts of the building and equipment in need of maintenance, repair, renovation, or replacement.

Church School Secretary

The responsibilities of the Church School Secretary are the following:

1. To see that adequate and accurate membership, attendance, and other specially designated records are maintained.
2. To see that class offerings are turned into the church's financial secretary.
3. To distribute communications and materials to superintendents and teachers on Sunday mornings.
4. To register new or visiting personnel on Sunday morning and direct them to the proper classes.
5. To keep the minutes for Church School staff meetings.

Department Superintendent

1. To assist the Church School Superintendent as directed in carrying out his responsibilities.
2. To see that departmental worship services are prepared and properly conducted.
3. To see that presentations are prepared for the regular departmental meetings.
4. To stimulate and coordinate out-of-the-classroom activities in the department.
5. To promote and participate in the home-and-church program.
6. To be alert to and report to the Superintendent all needs for improvement or expansion of instructional services.
7. To report to the Superintendent parts of the building and equipment in need of maintenance, repair, renovation or replacement.

Teachers

1. To maintain familiarity with the educational philosophy, objectives, plans, policies, and standards of the Church School and to work in accordance with them.
2. To maintain familiarity with the Church School curriculum and carry out instructional work in accordance with its outlines and objectives.

3. To maintain familiarity with the "Self-Rating Questionnaire for Church School Teachers" published in this handbook and to evaluate one's teaching regularly by this questionnaire.

4. To be present for teaching at all Sunday class sessions except for unavoidable causes such as illness, emergency calls out of town, or an annual vacation, about which the church office or superintendent of the department is notified in advance.

5. To be present at all faculty meetings.

6. To promote and participate in the home-and-church program.

7. To promote and participate in the parent-teacher group, regularly attending its meetings and activities.

8. To give adequate time and attention to the preparation of teaching sessions.

9. To give serious and regular attention to the matter of professional training and improvement.

10. To attend regularly the worship service of Bay Shore Community Church.

THIRTEEN

A Program for the Development of Potential Leadership

(Adult Elective Curriculum Program for Sunday Church School, Eagle Rock Baptist Church, Los Angeles, California.)

The following program is one which is used as a Sunday school curriculum for adults. This type of program often trains individuals sufficiently well so that they can eventually be recruited for teaching purposes. Its success is dependent upon the presence or procurement of several capable teachers who are creative enough to make up their own lecture notes or discussion materials.

A. Registration Information

ADULT DIVISION ELECTIVE CURRICULUM PROGRAM

Registration Form for the May-July Quarter Beginning May 5

(Return this completed form to the Sunday school or church offices)

Name: ....Phone:........................

Address: ....City:..............Zone:.............

Please Check Your

Class Social Unit: Adult........: Ambassador........: Fellowship........:

Clipper........: Berean........:

ELECTIVE CURRICULUM COURSES

(Indicate by numbers your first, second and third choices of classes)

Survey of the New Testament

Matt.-Phil.) ....Teacher ....

History of Christianity .... Teacher ....

The Book of Romans .... Teacher ....

On Being a Real Person .... Teacher ....

The Book of Job .... Teacher ....

Evangelism in Action .... Teacher ....

Every effort will be made to put every student in the first choice class, but in cases where this is not possible, the second and third choices will be used.

B. Instructions

THE ADULT DIVISION ELECTIVE EDUCATION CURRICULUM MAY-JULY QUARTER

THE ELECTIVE CURRICULUM PROGRAM

On the following pages you will find a description of the six courses to be taught in the first quarter, May-July 1963, of the new Adult Division Elective Education Program in the Sunday School of Eagle Rock Baptist Church.

Each quarter six different courses of study will be available. You will choose the course which is best for you. Many courses offered the first quarter will be available in future quarters, therefore all students may have a choice of most courses available.

The program is supervised by the Board of Christian Education of the Eagle Rock Baptist Church.

HOW THE PROGRAM WILL WORK

Present Sunday School Classes Remain Organized

The following adult Sunday school classes will remain organized for the purpose of providing mutual inspiration and fellowship: Single Adult, Ambassadors, Fellowship, Clipper, and Berean.

The Time Schedule

The social units will meet from 9:30 to 9:50 A.M. for the normal class activities. At 9:50 A.M. a passing bell will ring and all adults will move to their particular elective classrooms. Teaching time in the elective curricuum will be from 9:55 A.M. to 10:45 A.M. There will be a 15-minute period from the dismissal of the elective class to the morning worship hour, at 11:00 A.M. Under this schedule the student will have a full 50 minutes of vital instruction.

The Schedule: 9:30 - 9:50 A.M. — Social Units Meet
9:50 - 9:55 A.M. — Movement to Elective Classroom

203

9:55 - 10:45 A.M. — Elective Class
10:45 - 11:00 A.M. — Break Period
11:00 - 12:00 A.M. — Worship in the Sanctuary

HOW TO REGISTER

1. Secure a yellow registration form from the Sunday school or church office.

2. Read carefully the course descriptions and make your first, second and third choices. Because the classes must be held to about 30 students, it is evident that not all will be able to enroll in the class of their first choice. It is therefore important that a second and third choice be noted on the registration form.

3. Fill out the registration form completely and return to either office.

4. You will be notified as to the class that is open for you to attend.

C. Sample Course Description

*THE ADULT DIVISION ELECTIVE EDUCATION
CURRICULUM MAY-JULY QUARTER
COURSE DESCRIPTION*

COURSE: *SURVEY OF THE NEW TESTAMENT* — Matthew through Philippians.

INSTRUCTOR: ——— ———

I *Purpose of the Course*
To get a bird's-eye view of the Scriptures which will encourage the individual Christian to a deeper study on his own. The New Testament is the Christian's charter of life, and there should be new interest with each reading, especially if the method is varied. It should be read in units: shorter units (paragraphs) in order to be understood and retained.

II *Outline of the Course*
There are thirteen Sundays in the quarter. There are eleven books from Matthew through Philippians. We shall have one week for Introductory Study; a "Book of the Week" study; and then one Sunday for summary and evaluation at the end.

204

III *Method of the Course*

Mimeographed sheets will be distributed weekly, containing the name of the book, its scope, key chapter, key verse, key word, key thought, contents, character, spiritual thought, how Christ is seen, the writer, where written, when written, to whom written, subject, purpose as compared with other Gospels or books, Old Testament passages quoted or referred to, and an outline.

Questions will also be included which will be asked and discussed in class. The blackboard will be used frequently.

IV *Recommended Text*

The Bible only, for the present. Later, if a suitable inexpensive text is found, it may be recommended for class use to follow along.

> Adapted from mimeographed
> material of the Eagle Rock
> Baptist Church, Los Angeles,
> California

FOURTEEN

Biblical and Practical Studies Program for Youth

(Curricula and Courses for the Impact Program, Chevy Chase Baptist Church, Glendale, California.)

Majors

Students who desire to complete the work required for a diploma must first complete two years of fundamental studies covering all three fields of instruction, as listed in Chart I below. This training is designed to provide a general background in Biblical and church-related subjects. With this background behind him, the student may declare one or more majors. Majors are offered in Theology, Bible, and Organization-Administration. Each major requires one hour per week for an additional two years. If the student desires to continue during the summer quarter, he may take some of the various elective courses offered. If the student should desire to take a double major, he may do so by attending classes two days a week instead of the one day required for a single major. In any case the student should be counseled before declaring a major. The recommended courses for each major are listed below.

CHART I – FOUNDATIONAL

Area	Year I	Year II
Theology	Survey of Christian Doctrine	General Apologetics
Bible	Old Testament Survey	New Testament Survey
Organization and Administration	Techniques of Research	Basic Speech Techniques Speech Workshop

CHART II – THEOLOGY MAJOR

Year III	Year IV
Systematic Theology	Guided Research
Theology Seminar	Contemporary Problems in Theology

CHART III – BIBLE MAJOR

Year III	Year IV
General Biblical Introduction	Personal Evangelism
Analysis of Romans	Biblical Backgrounds
	Guided Research

CHART IV — ORGANIZATION AND ADMINISTRATION MAJOR

Year III
Intermediate Speech
Programing
Organization

Year IV
Psychology of Personality

Adapted from printed brochure
of Chevy Chase Baptist Church,
Glendale, California

FIFTEEN

Form Used in Worker Recruitment Procedure

(Sunday School Workers Standards and Covenant, Moody Church, Chicago, Illinois.)

Statement:

Recognizing the essential need of Christian education and my privilege and duty to render personal service to my Lord through the organized efforts of the Sunday school, I promise my Lord that I will be faithful in the discharge of my duties and responsibilities and agree to the following covenant:

1. I have received Jesus Christ as my Savior and Lord, and am now living in daily communion with Him. That God may show me how I may be of the greatest help to the Sunday school shall be my constant prayer.

2. I purpose to be present every Sunday. If it is necessary for me to be absent, I will notify the department superintendent as early in the week as possible.

3. Knowing the value of a good example, I will make it a practice to come on time to each session, and interpret this to mean I am to be present at least ten minutes before the opening of the school each Sunday, unless hindered by some reason I can conscientiously give to God.

4. As a worker in the Sunday school, I shall feel my responsibility toward the church and agree to attend all its services as regularly as possible, and I will use my influence to secure the attendance of the pupils of the Sunday school in church.

5. I will take time to prepare thoroughly for the teaching of each lesson if my responsibilities involve teaching, and will help by personal example to create an attitude of reverence and good behavior in the school.

6. I will attend regularly the meetings appointed for workers of the Sunday school, unless prevented by some reason I can conscientiously give to God.

7. I will earnestly strive and pray for the salvation of those members of my department who are not Christians and will

seek to lead them to accept Jesus Christ as their personal Savior.

8. I shall endeavor to keep complete and accurate records.

9. I shall endeavor by every possible means, such as visitation, telephone, and writing, to keep in touch with my pupils and secure their regular attendance.

10. I purpose to pray regularly for my class, department, and the whole work of the Sunday school and church, and shall attend the periods of united prayer set apart by my department or the school as a whole.

(For Sunday School Workers Only)

I have read the Moody Sunday School Workers' Standards and Covenant and signify that I am in full accord with them, subscribe to them, trusting in His grace for their fulfillment.

Date ....19........ Signed ....

Phone .... Address ....

SIXTEEN

Teacher Training Programs

(Teacher Training Institutes of the First Presbyterian Church, Hollywood, California.)

1. Sunday Program (Student is expected to attend church at the 9:30 hour and the Institute at 11:00):

February 24 - May 26, 1963
Sundays, 11:00 a.m.

(No Meetings Palm Sunday, Easter, Mother's Day)

Feb. 24 — The Teacher
Mar. 3 — The Bible, the Word of God
Mar. 10 — Old Testament Perspective
Mar. 17 — New Testament Perspective
Mar. 24 — Age Characteristics
Mar. 31 — Over-all View of Curriculum
Apr. 7 — Palm Sunday and Easter — No Meetings
Apr. 14 — Interviews — During Easter Vacation
Apr. 21 — Tools, Dictionaries, Encyclopedias, Translations,
      Commentaries
      11:00 a.m. — Discussion
Apr. 28 — 9:30 a.m. — Visit Area Want to Teach
May 5 — Pupil — Age Characteristics) Preschool 2-3
) Preschool 4-5
May 12 — Mothers' Day — No Meeting) Primary
) Junior
May 19 — How to Prepare a Lesson) Junior High
) Senior High
May 26 — Class Room Techniques
      Meeting Places to Be Announced Later

CHRISTIAN EDUCATION DEPARTMENT —
FIRST PRESBYTERIAN CHURCH OF HOLLYWOOD

Registration Form — Turn in to Christian Education Department

Name ....Address ....

City ....Zone.......Phone........................

Department Teaching .... Not Teaching Now ....

2. Week-Night Program (The monthly Teachers' and Officers' meeting offers some opportunity for teacher training. The following schedule might be used):

 5:15 - 6:15 p.m. — Sunday School Cabinet Meeting
 6:15 - 7:00 p.m. — Dinner for All Teachers and Officers
 7:00 - 7:20 p.m. — Minister Speaking on "Our Presbyterian Church"
 7:20 - 8:20 p.m. — Workshops:
  Pre school — "What About Our Three to Fives?"
  Primary — "Primaries Are Worshipers"
  Junior — "Making Your Lesson Live"
  Junior High — "Preparing Your Lesson"
  Senior High — "Our Greatest Asset"
  College — "The Personal Worker"
  Adults — "The Christian Family"
 8:20 - 9:30 p.m. — Departmental Executive Sessions

3. One-Day Conference

A One-Day Conference with special classes has proven successful in teacher training. A program such as the following might be used — (conference held at conference grounds, if possible):

 1:00 - 2:30 p.m. — Luncheon and address from visiting speaker
 2:30 - 3:15 p.m. — Get-acquainted time
 3:15 - 4:15 p.m. — Workshops:
  Pre school — Preschool expert
  Primary — Storyteller of renown
  Junior — Storyteller of renown
  Junior High — Superintendent in charge
  Senior High — Superintendent in charge
  Adult — Executive meetings
 4:30 - 5:30 p.m. — Missionary speaker
 6:00 - 7:00 p.m. — Dinner — Fun — Fellowship
 7:00 - 7:30 p.m. — Heart-to-heart talk, Minister of your church
 7:45 - 8:30 p.m. — Fun Time: Sunday school play or skit.

Adapted from mimeographed materials
of First Presbyterian Church, Hollywood,
California

SEVENTEEN

Church Calendar

(With meetings fixed on specific day of the week)

(Church Calendar, First Baptist Church, Fresno, California.)

The Lord's Day

Bible School Classes for All Ages .... 9:45 a.m.
Morning Worship Services .... 11:00 a.m.
Expanded Session of Bible School .... 11:00 a.m.
Communion Service (first Sunday of each month) 11:00 a.m.
Youth Council (second Sunday of each month) .... 4:00 p.m.
Challengers Choir Rehearsal .... 5:45 p.m.
Junior High Fellowship .... 6:15 p.m.
Challengers Junior Fellowship .... 6:15 p.m.
Senior High Fellowship .... 6:15 p.m.
College Age Fellowship .... 6:15 p.m.
Single Adult Fellowship .... 6:00 p.m.
The Sunday Evening Hour .... 7:30 p.m.

The Lord's Week

Monday

Scout Troop Meeting (every Monday) .... 7:00 p.m.
Amy Purcell Guild (first Monday) .... 7:30 p.m.
Rebecca Circle, Home of Members (second Monday) 8:00 p.m.
Business and Professional Women's Circle,
    Church Parlor (second Monday) .... 7:30 p.m.
Mary Circle, Home of Members (second Monday) 8:00 p.m.
J.O.Y. Circle, Home of Members (second Monday 7:30 p.m.
Men's Brotherhood (third Monday) .... 6:30 p.m.
Explorer Post Meeting (second and fourth Monday) 7:00 p.m.

Tuesday

Allied Arts (first Tuesday) .... 8:00 p.m.
Miriam Circle, Home of Members (second Tuesday) 9:30 a.m.
Esther, Ruth, Martha, Lydia, Naomi, Dorcas (afternoon
    circles) Homes of Members (second Tuesday .... 12:30 p.m.
Welcome Class (third Tuesday) .... 12:00 p.m.

Women's Mission Society (fourth Tuesday) .... 11:00 a.m.
    December and June Meetings on second Tuesday
Cub Pack Meeting (fourth Tuesday) .... 7:30 p.m.

Wednesday

Catered Dinner and Fellowship in Fellowship
Hall .... 6:00-7:15 p.m.
Bible Study and Prayer in Fellowship Hall ....7:15-7:45 p.m.
Activities for Children in Rooms 6, 7, 12 .... 7:45-8:30 p.m.
Study Courses in Rooms 8, 11, 15 .... 7:45-8:30 p.m.
Junior High Choir in Room 9 .... 7:45-8:30 p.m.

The following Boards and Committees meet on their scheduled
Wednesday night, 7:45-8:45 p.m.

1st Wednesday night
    Advisory Board — Church Parlor
    Library Committee — Library and Room 16
    Evangelism Committee and Training in Evangelism — Room 19

2nd Wednesday night
    Board of Deacons — Church Parlor
    Recreation Committee — Room 16
    Drama Club — Room 10
    Evangelistic Calling — Room 19

3rd Wednesday night
    Board of Trustees — Church Parlor
    New-Member Integration — Room 19

4th Wednesday night
    Board of Christian Education — Church Parlor
    Building Committee — Room 14
    New-Member Integration — Room 19

5th Wednesday night (quarterly)
    Bible School Workers' Conference — Church Parlor
    Committees of the Board of Deacons
    Committees of the Board of Trustees
    New-Member Integration — Room 19
    Evangelistic Calling — Room 19
    Nominating Committee — Room 8

213

The following Boards and Committees will meet on their scheduled Wednesday night quarterly, 7:45-8:45 p.m.

1st Wednesday (quarterly)

Leadership Education Committee — Room 14 — Feb., May, Nov.

Missionary Education Committee — Room 14 — Jan., April, Oct.

Visual Education Committee — Room 14 — March, June, Sept. Dec.

2nd Wednesday (quarterly)

Nursery Committee — Room 14 — Jan., April, Oct.

Higher Education Committee — Room 14 — Feb., May, Nov.

Scouting Committee — Room 14 — March, June, Sept., Dec.

3rd Wednesday (quarterly)

Children's Committee — Room 16 — Jan., April, Oct.

Youth Committee — Room 16 — Feb., May, Nov.

Adult Committee — Room 16 — March, Sept., Dec.

Thursday

Senior Choir Rehearsal .... 7:30 p.m.

Friday

Fidelity Club (first Friday) .... 7:30 p.m.
Seekers Class (third Friday) .... 7:00 p.m.
Friendship Class (fourth Friday) .... 7:00 p.m.

Saturday

King's Daughters Guild (second Saturday) .... 10:30 a.m.
Loyal Builders Class (fourth Saturday) .... 7:00 p.m.

EIGHTEEN

Coordination Through Communication Techniques

(Publications of the Department of Christian Education, Bay Shore Community Church, Long Beach, California.)

The following publications are based upon executive activities and are issued by the Minister of Christian Education (or are for him):

Executive Activity	Publication Issued	Purpose of Publication	To Whom Addressed	Frequency of Issue	Scheme by Which filed
Planning	Planning Bulletin	To inform of plans	Usually the Bd. of Chr. Ed.	As needed	By date
Directing	Memorandum	To communicate information to persons concerned.	Any member of the Dept.	As needed	By name of addressee
Co-ordinating	Handbook	Orientate all Dept. personnel and co-ordinate all activities.	All Dept. personnel	As needed	Kept as a unit in a loose-leaf binder
Stimulating	Newsletter	Stimulate activity by keeping all persons informed.	All Dept. personnel	Bi-weekly	By date
Evaluating	Report	Report progress of activities	Persons concerned with the information	As needed	By activity and date

NINETEEN

The Annual Report as a Technique of Control

(Report of the Board of Christian Education, Planning Conference Manual, Lake Avenue Congregational Church, Pasadena, California, 1956.)

The Board of Christian Education has conducted the various phases of its work during the first five months of the year with the evident blessing of God. Much of its activities are covered in the reports of the:

> Minister of Youth
>
> Pioneer Girls
>
> Boy Scouts
>
> Sunday School
>
> Christian Endeavor
>
> Missionary Committee

The Board serves to integrate the above activities.

Plans for the future include: D.V.B.S., the Sunday School Picnic, and the Fall Rally Banquet.

The effective ministry of the Library and Visual-Aids Department is an ever widening educational service. Sunday school teachers are rejoicing in the material aid received to do a better teaching job. Our present assets include 2,000 volumes and complete flannelgraph file of Bible lesson material. This was prepared by the librarian who spends several days a week in the library. The high circulation is seen in the figures for the first four months of the current year. 990 items were checked out, 142 of them flannelgraph lessons. The average number of books going out every month is 250. Eighty books have been purchased, 36 donated. During the period January 1 to May 9, $75.62 was spent for new books.

In the Visual-Aids Department: 60 backgrounds have been made; 70 overlays; 2,000 figures backed and cut out and filed; 3 flannel boards; between 800-900 slides for Sunday school use; 35 film strips (including hymns and stories); 20 records; 1 record player; and 300 pictures (large) have been backed; one portable typewriter.

The Board was happy to welcome the new leaders of Pioneer Girls from our church, as well as our new Assistant Sunday School Superintendent.

Adapted from the Planning
Conference Manual 1956, of
Lake Avenue Congregational Church,
Pasadena, California

TWENTY

Absentee Follow-Up Form

(Follow-Up Procedure Blank, Temple Baptist Church, Los Angeles, California.)

Absentee Follow-Up (To be returned to the Department Secretary next week).

Class ....Teacher (or Group Captain) ....Date........

ABSENT TWICE (to be phoned)

Name	Phone	Did You Phone?	Information Obtained	Other Contact
....
....
....

ABSENT THREE TIMES (to be visited)

Name	Address	Date Visit Made	Information Obtained	Other Contact
....
....
....

VISITORS (to be called on)

Name	Address	Phone	Information Obtained
....
....
....
....

Selected Bibliography

Items marked with an asterisk(*) are concerned primarily with the church and Christian education. The remaining items are drawn largely from the fields of education and business administration.

*Allen, Clifton J., and Howse, W. L. *The Curriculum Guide.* Nashville: Convention Press, 1960.

Allen, Louis A. *Management and Organization.* New York: McGraw-Hill, 1958.

American School Superintendency. American Association of School Administrators, Thirtieth Yearbook. Washington: American Association of School Administrators of the National Education Association, 1952.

Barnard, Chester I. *The Functions of the Executive.* Cambridge, Massachusetts: Harvard University Press, 1938.

*Barnette, J. N. *A Church Using Its Sunday School.* Nashville: Sunday School Board of the Southern Baptist Convention, 1937.

*Blackwood, Andrew W. *Pastoral Leadership.* Nashville: Abingdon-Cokesbury Press, 1949.

*Burkhart, Roy A. *How the Church Grows.* New York: Harper and Brothers, 1947.

*Butler, J. Donald. *Religious Education.* New York: Harper and Row, 1962.

*Crossland, Weldon. *How to Build Up Your Church School.* New York: Abingdon-Cokesbury Press, 1948.

Dalton, Melville. *Men Who Manage.* New York: John Wiley and Sons, 1959.

219

DeHuzar, George. *Practical Applications of Democracy.* New York: Harper and Brothers, 1945.

Department of the Air Force. *Management Course for Air Force Supervisors.* Washington, D.C.: U.S. Government Printing Office, 1955.

*Department of Children's Work, Board of Education and Publication. *Vacation Church School Handbook.* Philadelphia: American Baptist Convention, 1703 Chestnut Street, Philadelphia 3, Pennsylvania, 1954.

*Division of Christian Education. *The Organization and Administration of Christian Education in the Local Church.* Chicago: National Council of the Churches of Christ in the United States of America, 1951.

*Dobbins, Gaines S. *Building Better Churches.* Nashville: Broadman Press, 1947.

*Dolloff, Eugene Dinsmore. *A Crowded Church.* New York: Fleming H. Revell, 1946.

Dubin, Robert. *Human Relations in Administration.* New York: Prentice-Hall, 1951.

Executive Life. Editors of Fortune. Garden City: Doubleday and Company, 1956.

Executive Office of the President, Bureau of the Budget, "Production Planning and Control in Office Operations," Management Bulletin, October, 1949, Superintendent of Documents, U.S. Government Printing Office, Washington 25, D.C.

*Fairchild, Roy W., and Wynn, John C. *Families in the Church.* New York: Association Press, 1961.

*Gable, Lee J. *Christian Nurture Through the Church.* New York: National Council of Churches, 1955.

Gill, William A. "Survey Principles and Techniques," reprint from *Modern Management.* Available from the author, William A. Gill, P.O. Box 3025, Alexandria, Virginia.

Goldwin, Robert, and Nelson, Charles A. (eds.). *Toward the Liberally Educated Executive.* New York: The New American Library of World Literature, 501 Madison Avenue, New York, 1960.

Gordon, Thomas. *Group-Centered Leadership.* Cambridge: Houghton Mifflin, 1955.

Goulder, Alvin W. (ed.). *Studies in Leadership.* New York: Harper and Brothers, 1950.

Gulick, Luther Halsey, and Urwick, L. (eds.). *Papers on the Science of Administration.* New York: Institute of Public Administration, Columbia University, 1937.

*Heim, Ralph D. *Leading a Sunday Church School.* Philadelphia: Muhlenberg Press, 1950.
Henry, Nelson B. (ed.). *Changing Conceptions in Educational Administration.* Chicago: University of Chicago Press, 1946.

Laird, Donald A. and Eleanor C. *The Techniques of Delegating.* New York: McGraw-Hill, 1957.
*Landis, Benson Y. (ed.). *Edition for 1956 Yearbook of American Churches.* New York: Office of Publication and Distribution, National Council of Churches of Christ in the U.S.A., 1955.
*———— *Edition for 1962 Yearbook of American Churches.* New York: Office of Publication and Distribution, National Council of Churches of Christ in the U.S.A., 1961.
*Leach, William H. *Handbook of Church Management.* Englewood Cliffs: Prentice-Hall, 1956.
Leadership in American Education. Proceedings of Cooperative Conference for Administrators of Public and Private Schools, Vol. XIII. Compiled and edited by Alonzo G. Grace. Chicago: Chicago Press, 1950.
*Lobingier, John L. *The Better Church School.* Boston: Pilgrim Press, 1952.
*Lotz, Philip Henry. *Orientation in Religious Education.* Nashville: Abingdon-Cokesbury Press, 1950.

*McCann, Richard V. *The Churches and Mental Health.* New York: Basic Books, 1961.
*Miller, Randolph C. *Education for Christian Living.* Englewood Cliffs: Prentice-Hall, 1956.
Miller, Van (ed.). *Providing and Improving Administrative Leadership for America's Schools.* New York: Bureau of Publications, Teachers College, Columbia University, 1951.
Miller, Van, and Spalding, Willard B. *The Public Administration of American Schools.* New York: World Book Co., Yonkers-on-Hudson, N.Y., 1952.
Moehlman, Arthur B. *School Administration.* Boston: Houghton Mifflin, 1951.
Mooney, James D. *The Principles of Organization* (Revised Edition). New York: Harper and Brothers, 1947.

Mort, Paul R. *Principles of School Administration.* New York: McGraw-Hill, 1946.

National Education Association. *Moral and Spiritual Values in the Public Schools.* Washington, D.C.: National Education Association, 1951.

Newman, William H. *Administrative Action.* New York: Prentice-Hall, 1951.

Pfiffner, John M., and Sherwood, Frank P. *Administrative Organization.* Englewood Cliffs: Prentice-Hall, 1960.

Pfiffner, John. *The Supervision of Personnel.* Englewood Cliffs: Prentice-Hall, 1958.

*Pleuthner, Willard A. *Building Up Your Congregation.* Chicago: Wilcox and Follett Co., 1950.

*Preston, Mary Frances Johnson. *Christian Leadership.* Nashville: Sunday School Board of the Southern Baptist Convention, 1934.

*Price, J. M., Carpenter, L., and Chapman, J. H. *Introduction to Religious Education.* New York: Macmillan Co., 1932.

Reeder, Ward G. *Fundamentals of Public School Administration.* New York: Macmillan Co., 1951.

Reeves, Floyd W. "Some General Principles of Administrative Organization," *Current Issues in Library Administration.* Edited by Carleton B. Joeckel. Chicago: University of Chicago Press, 1939.

*Richardson, Alan. *An Introduction to the Theology of the New Testament.* New York: Harper and Brothers, 1958.

Russell, John Dale. *The Finance of Higher Education.* Chicago: University of Chicago Bookstore, University of Chicago, 1946.

Schleh, Edward C. *Successful Executive Action.* Englewood Cliffs: Prentice-Hall, 1955.

Sears, Jesse B. *The Nature of the Administrative Process.* New York: McGraw-Hill, 1950.

*Sherrill, Lewis J. *The Gift of Power.* New York: Macmillan Co., 1959.

Simon, Herbert A. *Administrative Behavior.* New York: Macmillan Co., 1957.

*Smart, James. *Teaching Ministry of the Church.* Philadelphia: Westminster Press, 1954.

Sorenson, Roy. *The Art of Board Membership.* New York: Association Press, 1953.
*Special Committee on the Curriculum Guide Division of Christian Education. *A Guide for Curriculum in Christian Education.* Chicago: National Council of Churches of Christ in the U.S.A., 1955.

*Taylor, Marvin J. *Religious Education.* Nashville: Abingdon Press, 1960.
Tead, Ordway. *The Art of Administration.* New York: McGraw-Hill Co., 1951.
Trecker, Harleigh B. *Group Process in Administration.* New York: The Women's Press, 1947.

Upson, Lent D. *Letters on Public Administration.* Detroit: Citizens Research Council of Michigan, 810 Farwell Building, Detroit 26, Michigan, 1954.
Urwick, Lyndall. *Elements of Administration.* New York: Harper and Brothers, 1944.

*Vieth, Paul H. *Church School.* Philadelphia: Christian Education Press, 1957.

*Wyckoff, D. Campbell. *How to Evaluate Your Christian Education Program.* Philadelphia: Westminster Press, 1962.

Yauch, Wilbur A. *Improving Human Relations in School Administration.* New York: Harper and Brothers, 1949.

Index

225